The Earning Organization™ Series

REINVENT *YOUR* ENTERPRISE
Through Better Knowledge Work

by Jack Bergstrand

Founder, Brand Velocity, Inc.

ISBN: 1-4392-1985-0

ISBN-13: 9781439219850

Library of Congress Control Number: 2008911069

Visit www.amazon.com to order additional copies.

Talent hits a target no one else can hit;
Genius hits a target no one else can see.

—Arthur Schopenhauer
German philosopher 1788-1860

REINVENT *YOUR* ENTERPRISE

Through Better Knowledge Work

TABLE OF CONTENTS

REINVENT *YOUR* ENTERPRISE

FOREWORD

On one level, *Reinvent Your Enterprise* is as straightforward as it could be. Just as its title implies, it'll teach you how to refashion your company—specifically, with an eye toward tackling what Peter Drucker identified as the greatest challenge of the 21st century: enhancing knowledge worker productivity.

Ever prescient, Drucker coined the term "knowledge worker" in 1959, when about a third of U.S. employees were still engaged in manufacturing (compared with only 1 in 10 today). He spent much of the next 40-plus years writing about *what* managers need to do in an era that demands we use our brains more than our backs, our heads more than our hands. Among other steps, Drucker called for giving knowledge workers sufficient autonomy and treating employees as assets rather than as costs. Jack Bergstrand's remarkable contribution is to explain *how* businesses should actually go about doing these things.

But on a different level, this book is about something else—something much bigger. At the core of Drucker's philosophy is the notion that when organizations fail to perform, we all suffer. "The well-being of our entire society," he wrote, "depends increasingly on the ability of . . . large numbers of knowledge workers to be effective."

So, go ahead and reinvent your enterprise. Along the way, you may just wind up reinventing society as well.

Rick Wartzman

Director
The Drucker Institute
Claremont Graduate University
Claremont, California

Introduction: Reinvent *Your* Enterprise

"Today, the majority of U.S. workers are employed in the services sector, and knowledge has become our most important product. According to the United States Chamber of Commerce, 75% of our workforce consists of managerial, professional, service, sales, and office workers. With our fast computers, sophisticated software, and high-speed networks, many hoped that knowledge work productivity would grow naturally and rapidly. Unfortunately, it hasn't. Instead, we have gotten stuck and the productivity paradox has been the result."

INTRODUCTION

Peter F. Drucker emphasized for decades that improving knowledge work productivity needed to be the next management frontier [1-4]. In fact, he was convinced that our prosperity and even our economic survival depend on it [5]. Unfortunately, we are living with an interrelated set of economic and social challenges resulting from the "productivity paradox," which is the *lack* of productivity improvement that experts have struggled to explain despite more than a generation of large information technology investments and price/performance improvements. To increase corporate performance and economic prosperity, it is clear that a better and more systematic management approach is needed. Fortunately, the system for managing knowledge work productivity that Drucker recommended is also an excellent mechanism for sustainable Enterprise reinvention.

It's time to begin reinventing our Enterprises through better knowledge work. This will require a new and more systematic approach to serve customers better, improve corporate integration, and accelerate key Enterprise projects. This is no small matter. According to the Project Management Institute, $12 trillion—nearly 20% of the world's GDP—is invested in projects. Yet, because we have not yet been able to systematically improve knowledge work productivity, we continue to suffer from high Enterprise project failure rates.

This book was written to help business people begin the journey to systematically improve knowledge work productivity and, in so doing, create more successful companies and a better society. To achieve this, *Reinvent Your Enterprise* combines extensive research—more than 50,000 pages and nearly 250 references—with lessons learned during thirty years of personal experience in large and small companies.

As part of this book's research, fundamental knowledge work productivity principles were prototyped with employees and customers over a five-year period. In addition, a knowledge work productivity system and a survey-based tool was developed, implemented, and refined in practice—to help you move your Enterprise forward better and faster.

Many companies struggle because they haven't been able to successfully manage their knowledge work productivity [1-3, 6] even though the number knowledge workers has grown substantially over time. An important cause of this problem, and a recurring theme in this book, is that knowledge work management has been constrained to a significant degree by the same scientific methods that helped companies successfully manage manual work for much of the 20th century.

To help business people solve this management challenge, *Reinvent Your Enterprise* integrates practice, theory, prototypes, and tools. In so doing, this book greatly benefits from the insights of hundreds of management and social science scholars. They include Peter Drucker from Claremont [1] who did more than anyone to emphasize the importance of better and faster knowledge work, Peter Senge from M.I.T. [7] who put systems thinking on the map for managers of my generation, Thomas Davenport from Babson College [8] who has beautifully articulated so many important knowledge work ideas, and David Schwandt [9] from The George Washington University who opened my eyes to many applicable social science insights.

Building on that foundation, the rest of this introduction focuses on and integrates four areas to provide context for all ten chapters of *Reinvent Your Enterprise*:

- Reconstructing experience

- The link between reinvention, productivity, and prosperity

- Creating a better system for knowledge work productivity

- Reinvention—a corporate and societal choice

Reconstructing experience

This book is influenced by my background, and reconstructing my experience is an important factor in how *Reinvent Your Enterprise* is organized. I've integrated large and small company experiences in this book to guard against the danger of being like the parenting expert who has never had children.

In the corporate world, I worked for more than twenty years in the Coca-Cola system, where among other jobs I ran The Coca-Cola Company's global information technology function until 2001. To this day, I believe that nothing in large Enterprises exposes the function and sometimes the dysfunction of knowledge work better than large technology projects. I was also chief financial officer and head of manufacturing and logistics for the publicly traded Canadian bottler, Coca-Cola Beverages, during a high profile turnaround period in the 1990s. This influenced my thinking on productive knowledge work—when necessity frequently became the mother of invention. Prior to that, I was on the due diligence team for the formation of Coca-Cola Enterprises in the late 1980s, which for more than two decades has been the largest bottling company in the world. During my time there I led the corporate distribution function, was general manager of a division, and chief marketing officer for one of the company's major markets. I thoroughly enjoyed my corporate career.

My large company experiences taught me many valuable lessons about what works and what doesn't—up, down, and across complex organizational hierarchies. I also learned a lot during my time in the Coca-Cola system about both Enterprise change and Enterprise inertia. While I will draw upon examples from my corporate experience to illustrate points throughout this book, *Reinvent Your Enterprise* isn't a collection of Coca-Cola war stories. And, while this global corporate experience was valuable, it certainly didn't provide a total picture for how to best invent and reinvent Enterprises through better and faster knowledge work.

In addition to working in the Coca-Cola system, being founder and CEO of a start-up company contributed greatly to the thinking in this book. Starting a company from a clean sheet of paper—based on knowledge work productivity principles—has been a great eye opener. I've been fortunate to be able to work with a wide variety of interesting clients and a wonderful group of colleagues. This experience has clearly improved the content of this book, solidifying what works in a variety of situations across a broad base of companies.

A third important influence on this book came from the academic community. I owe a debt of gratitude to The George Washington, Stanford, and Michigan State universities. A master's degree in advertising management at MSU helped me understand the power of integrating business and communications. A master's degree in management from Stanford provided me with an intense yet traditional business education. It also helped me appreciate the sheer knowledge work productivity power of Silicon Valley, where brainpower and financial capital often work together as if they are one thing [10-14]. Finally, doctoral work in executive leadership at The George

Washington University provided key social science insights into knowledge work and how to improve Enterprises as social constructions.

Nearly a century ago, educational scholar John Dewey [15] wrote that learning and growth come from reconstructing experience. Certainly this has been true for me. It is also clear that Enterprise reinvention requires that we reconstruct organizations from a knowledge work productivity perspective. The more sustainable our reconstructions, the more success we can expect. This will become clearer throughout the book.

The link between reinvention, productivity, and prosperity

Efficiency focuses on doing things right, effectiveness concentrates on doing the right things, and productivity is about doing them both at the same time. Productivity improvement, through inventing and reinventing Enterprises, is what generates the surpluses that pay for our standard of living.

Unfortunately, many of our Enterprises and institutions have gotten stuck from a productivity perspective. As a result, they have not been able to generate vital economic surpluses. At the national level, for example, the United States government has incurred trade and budget deficits for generations. In addition, many established companies have struggled to produce sustainable rates of revenue and profit growth. Finally, millions of consumers have accumulated more debt than they can repay.

The case for reinvention is compelling and urgent. And, as Sir Winston Churchill rightfully pointed out, to improve is to change and to be perfect is to change often. This applies to individuals, companies, and societies. If you are a pure capitalist, Enterprise reinvention is good because it can make people rich. If you have a purely social orientation, reinvention is good because productive businesses are the economic engines that fund modern societies. It's clear that there is a lot to fix—including our national and global financial infrastructure, budget and trade deficits, healthcare system, educational challenges, energy and water distribution problems, global warming, and homeland security vulnerabilities.

Unfortunately, insufficient knowledge work productivity has been a known problem with an unknown solution for more than a generation. Drucker emphasized the problem for decades. More recently, and well before the global financial meltdown in late 2008, Federal Reserve chairman Ben Bernanke warned U.S. leaders that if nothing changes in the United States, health and Social Security spending alone will create a cycle of rising debt and interest payments that will lead to fiscal crisis [16].

Solving the knowledge work productivity problem will require that we capitalize on the symbiotic relationship between business and society upon which we all depend. Strong and growing companies are needed to fund effective social structures, and effective social structures are needed to support the human and market needs of strong and growing companies. Given this interdependency, we need to reinvent our Enterprises. Not only for investors, but for everyone who works to make our companies and societies function.

Many of our economic and social issues are symptoms of the knowledge work productivity problem. To get unstuck, we will need to reinvent our Enterprises and improve our productivity as individuals, functions, and organizations. Most important, we will need to improve systematically and sustainably [7, 17-19].

Creating a better system for knowledge work productivity

For more than two centuries, productivity improvements have funded our personal, corporate, and national prosperity. By continually producing goods and services with less effort [20-22], more people have been able to afford more products and services, and this has benefited consumers and producers alike.

Healthy and sustainable productivity does not exploit or oppress. It rewards those who create it [23]. Therefore, leaders—including executives, teachers, labor leaders, and politicians—serve everyone's interests when they communicate that productivity improvements are good. Overall and over time these improvements benefit individuals, families, companies, and nations alike.

Better productivity generates the economic surpluses that pay wages, produce profits, and generate the tax revenues that support our social structures. If wages stay the same and productivity goes down, even flat wages will not be affordable for long. At the same time, if productivity were to go up 100%, wages could go up dramatically and continue to be very affordable.

Due to knowledge work productivity constraints, many managers have been forced to focus on the cost-oriented nature of efficiency instead of the wealth-generating nature of productivity. There is a clear difference between these two approaches. Efficiency focuses on inputs and tries to reduce them whereas productivity concentrates on outputs and tries to increase them. Cost cutting does not drive productivity. Reinvention does. It's not enough for companies to tighten their belts. We need to redesign our structures.

Many established companies have gotten stuck in cost cutting spirals because they have, from a systems perspective, hit a knowledge work productivity wall [6, 24-27]. Problems like this occur with every system and should be expected and then overcome. All systems can take their users only so far before they become constrained [17, 19, 26, 28, 29]. Then, those systems need to be replaced by the next generation.

Consider personal transportation from a systems perspective. On the lower end of the spectrum, people can rollerblade only so fast and so far before they are constrained by their ability to skate—both in terms of speed and distance. Being chased by a Doberman may make a person go faster for a while, but even then their skating will reach a limit. People can break through the rollerblade system constraint by riding a bicycle to go faster and farther, but still there is a limit. Then, they can break through the constraint of the bicycle with a car until it reaches its limit, and then they can use an airplane, which also has a limit. Every system eventually reaches a limit for a given purpose.

For centuries, our predecessors have been able to increase prosperity by breaking through productivity system limits. Farming was more productive than hunting, and manufacturing was more productive than farming. These productivity improvements—as people migrated from hunting to farming, and then from the farm to the factory—funded the personal and national wealth increases in our most economically developed countries. In the last century, for example, the percentage of agricultural workers in the United States shifted from 85% to 3% of the population. In the last fifty years manufacturing workers shifted from over 70% to less than 5%. The productivity improvements from these shifts have increased the prosperity of America and the rest of the economically developed world for many generations.

Today, the majority of U.S. workers are employed in the services sector, and knowledge has become our most important product. According to the United States Chamber of Commerce, 75% of our workforce consists of managerial, professional, service, sales, and office workers. With our fast computers, sophisticated software, and high-speed networks, many hoped that knowledge work productivity would grow naturally and rapidly. Unfortunately, it hasn't [1, 3, 6]. Instead, we have gotten stuck and the productivity paradox has been the result.

It's now clear that the speed of information and the productivity of knowledge work are two different things. The troubling fact is that we are a nation full of knowledge workers, and we have not been able to productively manage these organizational resources. The same techniques that work effectively for manual work have proven to be ineffective with knowledge work. Due to this disconnect, it doesn't matter how many computers we throw at the problem.

Peter Drucker warned managers, consultants, academics, and government officials for decades that we were in danger. He made it clear that for the prosperity of the developed world to continue—let alone grow— we need to systematically break through the knowledge work productivity wall [1, 3]. We have made massive investments in technology for decades but the math ultimately doesn't work, and pushing the old Scientific Management system harder isn't sufficient. A better management system is required.

Just as our ancestors successfully broke through the productivity constraints of hunting versus farming and farming versus manufacturing, we now need to do the same with knowledge work. Manufacturing achieved a 50-fold increase in productivity in the 20th century [3]. What can we do for an encore?

It has never been clearer. There is nothing more important from an economic and social perspective than improving knowledge work productivity. This requires that we reinvent our Enterprises [30] in the Knowledge Age.

Reinvention—a corporate and societal choice

An Enterprise is an economic choice to achieve something collectively that can't be accomplished by an individual. To be sustainable, Enterprises need to generate surpluses for workers as well as for the firms that employ them [31]. This requires a systematic approach [7], and from a design perspective [32, 33], needs to factor in that bad systems produce bad behaviors, good systems create good behaviors [17, 18, 31], and similar systems generate similar results.

The most productive way to improve the prosperity of our Enterprises is to change the structures that drive their performance. This requires reinvention. Similar to the symbiotic relationship between strong companies and strong societies, knowledge work productivity is needed to reinvent our Enterprises. Then those reinvented companies are needed to increase the firm's value on a sustainable basis.

Improving knowledge work productivity is our most important economic opportunity and the most important management challenge of the 21st century. If you are a corporate executive or board member, reinventing your Enterprise will be a critical to your success. If you are a politician or labor leader, your help to reinvent Enterprises will also be important for those who trust you to represent their short and long-term interests. If you're an individual knowledge worker, you are the source of this reinvention.

Productivity improvement and Enterprise change are at the heart of improving the performance of our companies, funding our current societies, and paying for the societies we want to have in the future.

Converted into a formula, productivity equals output divided by input. Since knowledge is an input that can be used and kept at the same time, knowledge work has the potential to generate the greatest productivity levels ever. On the other hand, knowledge has a short shelf life and the speed of application matters much more with knowledge work than with traditional manual work.

Drucker emphasized that economic growth [4] requires that managers simultaneously make their present Enterprises more effective, identify and realize their potential, and create different Enterprises for a different future [34]. In so doing, business leaders need to continually shift resources from less productive to more productive areas [35] through better and faster Enterprise reinvention.

There is clearly much to gain from Enterprise reinvention and a lot to lose if organizations can't get unstuck. People will naturally disagree on how the productivity paycheck gets distributed, but we can't deny that better knowledge work productivity will inevitably be the source of this paycheck. This is the most important economic and management challenge of our era. If we can improve knowledge work productivity anywhere near the extent to which our predecessors increased manual work productivity, we are at the threshold of an economic expansion in the 21st century, the likes of which we have never seen.

Chapter One: Transitioning From Manual Work to Knowledge Work

"Does it take your large company a couple of weeks to set up a meeting with key people because their calendars are so busy or because they won't be in the office for awhile? And even then, is it difficult to get contentious tradeoffs made and decisions acted upon? If so, you are either in trouble or headed toward it. It has never been clearer. Unless your company is a monopoly, if your Enterprise can't improve its knowledge work productivity and reinvent itself faster, your firm's best years are behind it."

Chapter One

TRANSITIONING FROM MANUAL WORK TO KNOWLEDGE WORK

This chapter begins with the question, what is knowledge work productivity and why is it important? I first read about knowledge workers in 1993 in Peter Drucker's book, *Post-Capitalist Society*. He had been speaking and writing about it for decades, but the term was new to me at that time. It's still not discussed often enough in business circles. Management scholar and consultant Thomas Davenport surfaced this after he authored *Thinking for a Living* in 2005 [8], and even posed on his blog the question, "Was Drucker Wrong?" [6]

Drucker's core message was that the economy used to run on manual work. Now, it runs on knowledge work. Knowledge work, which accounts for and generates the largest number of jobs, must be made more productive for our workers, companies and societies to maintain and improve their prosperity.

Knowledge work is how individuals and groups use ideas, expertise, information, and relationships to get things done. It includes tasks such as brainstorming, analysis, project management, and personal coaching. Knowledge work *productivity* is the effectiveness and efficiency of these tasks. To illustrate, people who are farmers, truck drivers, and assembly line workers are manual workers. They work hard for a living, and when they finish their day, it's visibly clear what they've accomplished. People who are researchers, analysts, and managers are knowledge workers. They also work hard for a living. However, when knowledge workers finish *their* day, their achievements are not always as clear. In fact, because of the ever-changing nature of knowledge work, it's conceivable for them to work all day on something that was important in the morning but no longer important by dinner time.

Even though knowledge work can be highly productive, the nature of the work has made it difficult to manage systematically using tools that were designed for manual work. For one thing, the work is largely invisible because much of it happens in people's heads. For another, consistent with Parkinson's Law and the Peter Principle, which are described further in Chapter Seven, knowledge work tends to expand to fill the time available, staff tends to accumulate, and knowledge workers sometimes rise to their level of incompetence [36, 37]. Like the old advertising adage, half of a company's knowledge work is wasted but it's often difficult to know which half.

Inextricably linked to the knowledge work productivity problem is the information technology productivity problem. Referred to as the productivity paradox, and attributed to Nobel Laureate economist Robert Solow, large investments in information technology have unfortunately contributed very little to our productivity. In the same way that knowledge work has often expanded to fill the time available, digital information has expanded to fill our available computational, storage, and bandwidth capacity. The main tool of the knowledge worker, the computer, and knowledge workers themselves have struggled to be productive even though both possess astonishing potential in this area.

Improving knowledge work productivity has so far been difficult. How do you manage Enterprise productivity when people go to meetings, analyze data, answer emails, talk on the phone, do research, write a report, interview a potential employee, make a presentation, or sit in their office to come up with a new idea? With manual work, when waste is generated, it is seen by everyone. With knowledge work, when effort is wasted, it's not nearly as visible. Just as with farming, manufacturing, and truck driving, there needs to be a litmus test for productive knowledge work. Ultimately, these results should be judged based on whether one of the following occurs:

- When something successful that never existed previously is now up and running.

- When something successful that existed previously has been improved or expanded.

- When something unsuccessful that existed previously has been stopped.

The productivity realized by achieving one of these three outputs can then be judged based on the speed with which it is accomplished and the cost required to finish the job. This needs to be managed systematically to accelerate change, reduce costs, and improve sustainable results. It is central to achieving better performance *from* your company, building more fun *into* your company, and—as a byproduct over time—creating a better society. Making the successful transition from productive manual work in the 20th century to productive knowledge work in the 21st century requires thinking about and synthesizing several key areas:

- The nature of manual work

- The nature of knowledge work

- The economics of the next wave

- Moving from manual work to knowledge work productivity

- Factoring in the difference between information and knowledge

- Reinventing Enterprises using a knowledge work productivity management system

The nature of manual work

Manual work productivity in manufacturing improved 5,000% in the 20th century. This 50-fold improvement generated much of the prosperity that the developed world takes for granted today [1]. Frederick Taylor [21], a mechanical engineer, started the manual work productivity movement [1, 34] through his work on Scientific Management in the early 1900s. Two important contributions of Scientific Management were standardizing how to take waste out of the manual work process and how to pay manual workers according to their productivity level.

Taylor's scientific approach helped improve the visible, specialized, and stable nature of manual work. He simplified jobs so that workers could be trained to perform various jobs in the most efficient way. Using objective processes and measures and formally allocating time for managers to plan the work of their employees, Taylor saw to it that standardized methods were established and rigorously followed.

Taylor's Scientific Management practices worked very well, and continue to work well, for the visible and stable nature of manual work. Unfortunately, they are not as effective with knowledge work, which requires a more holistic and dynamic management approach [19, 26].

The nature of knowledge work

Manual work is visible, specialized, and stable, whereas knowledge work is invisible, holistic, and ever changing. Unlike manual workers, knowledge workers use their situational knowledge to get things done in a dynamic environment. They tend to be formally educated and are often called on to run *and* change their organizations simultaneously.

Knowledge workers acquire knowledge through a combination of education, experience, and personal interaction and then use that knowledge to achieve organizational goals in changing environments. This work is generally much more project oriented than manual work. It is also more holistic because Enterprise productivity depends on one knowledge area being rapidly transferred to another. Finally, being able to solve a continually changing series of bottlenecks is important because a delay in one part of the work can often keep everything associated with it from moving forward.

Because of the invisible and ever-changing nature of the work, knowledge workers are sometimes not held to the same results-oriented standards as manual workers. But, they need to be. Knowledge work that doesn't systematically result in tangible output wastes scarce resources. Studies and projects that don't get implemented are a waste of time and money. Good ideas that are not implemented also waste resources. With the rapid half-life of knowledge, good ideas won't be good for long, even in the best circumstances [38, 39]. For this reason speed matters with knowledge work much more than with manual work.

Knowledge work actually needs to be managed better than manual work because there are so many ways for it to go off track and so many places for knowledge workers to hide. A few common examples of unproductive knowledge work include:

- Too many meetings that produce too few decisions and actions

- Competing internal priorities with no mechanism for resolution

- Studies that are completed and put on the shelf

- Projects that get started but are never finished

- Projects that get started but are not finished on time

- Projects that never get started but get talked about every year

- High executive turnover that causes frequent changes in direction

Knowledge work is difficult for Enterprises to manage because of its tendency to expand to fill the available time [37] in conjunction with organizational disconnects within and across hierarchies [36, 40]. To productively manage the invisible and elastic nature of knowledge work better, Drucker advised that we address it more systematically. He emphasized that Enterprises need to remove unproductive work and restructure work as part of an overall system to create a satisfied customer. In this light he believed that knowledge should be organized through teams, with clarity around who is in charge at what time, for what reason, and for how long [2, 3].

To manage knowledge work more productively, it's important to contrast the differences between Taylor's thinking on manual work with Drucker's on knowledge work:

Frederick Taylor on Manual Work	Peter Drucker on Knowledge Work
Define the task	Understand the task
Command and control	Give Autonomy
Strict standards	Continuous innovation
Focus on quantity	Focus on quality
Measure performance to strict standard	Continuously learn and teach
Minimize cost of workers for a task	Treat workers as an asset not a cost

These differences help explain why Enterprises have struggled when applying manual work management techniques to knowledge work. The same system that helped us get to where we are today with manual work has kept us from getting to where we need to go with knowledge work.

The economics of the next wave

Knowledge needs to be directed, organized, and then put into action [41] to improve Enterprises. The economic potential for knowledge work productivity success in the 21st century is significant. Consider the following example highlighting the financial leverage associated with improving long term Enterprise performance:

Imagine a company with the following characteristics:

- $1 billion in annual sales

- Earns 20% operating profits—$200 million

- Pays 35% of those profits in taxes—$ 70 million

- Is valued at 10 times its after-tax earnings—$1.3 billion

The yearly implications of a 10% financial improvement for this company are:

- $20 million more operating profit

- $130 million increase in market value

- Tax base increase of $7 million

In the 20th century, manual work productivity for manufacturing increased 50-fold. It is mind boggling to imagine what could happen if companies improved their growth and performance 50-fold in the 21st century.

The implications of a 21st century 50-fold increase for a $1 billion company:

- $9.8 billion more in annual operating profit

- $63.7 billion more in market value

- Annual tax contribution of $3.43 billion more

Breaking through the productivity barrier [1, 3, 6] and reinventing Enterprises [1-3, 34, 35, 42, 43] on a sustainable basis in the 21st century is an unprecedented long term corporate and societal opportunity. On the other hand, the implications are frightening if Enterprises don't or can't become more productive on a sustainable basis.

If the same $1 billion company has trouble competing in the global marketplace, its operating profit, income tax payment, and market value will fall rapidly—far faster than revenues. This threat of failure is concerning because many of our companies are stuck, and the pace of global competition is accelerating. In our global market, wherever you are locally, you increasingly need to be competitive globally [5]. Companies no longer compete only with the firm down the street. In many cases it's necessary to be competitive with every other Enterprise around the world.

The next frontier of management must deliver improvements in speed to compete globally. In the 21st century large firms won't threaten smaller companies nearly as much as fast companies will threaten slower ones. Since 1960, to reach critical mass, it took cable television twenty-five years, video-cassette recorders nine years, and the World-Wide-Web five years. Companies currently compete in the Google-Facebook-YouTube-Skype age where a new idea can be adopted technically on a global basis in less time than it takes to get a good night's sleep.

Does it take your large company a couple of weeks to set up a meeting with key people because their calendars are so busy or because they won't be in the office for awhile? And even then, is it difficult to get contentious tradeoffs made and decisions acted upon? If so, you are either in trouble or headed toward it. It has never been clearer. Unless your company is a monopoly, if your Enterprise can't improve its knowledge work productivity and reinvent itself faster, your firm's best years are behind it.

Moving from manual work to knowledge work productivity

For Enterprises to successfully make the transition to the knowledge work productivity world, it helps to think about knowledge work in the context of manual work [9, 27, 44-48]. One important similarity is that the goal of both is to create the biggest surplus possible given the available resources. With respect to differences, for one thing, the potential surplus for knowledge work productivity is much larger. At the same time, the shelf life of knowledge is shorter. These two countervailing forces change the rules of the productivity game.

To illustrate this further, think about the job of dog walkers in large cities such as New York. These enterprising people earn money by charging customers per dog, and it's amazing how many dogs a single person can walk at one time. In the tradition of Frederick Taylor, when dog walkers walk more dogs, they increase their productivity. These productivity increases generate greater surpluses for workers limited by how many dogs a person can walk.

Meanwhile, in Omaha, Nebraska, in the world of knowledge work, there is Warren Buffett. During much of my lifetime Mr. Buffett [49, 50] has been one of the richest, if not the richest, humans in the world [51]. In his case, he generated great wealth by being an extraordinarily successful and productive knowledge worker. As a result, he amassed a very large financial surplus.

Earning this amount of money as a manual worker is impossible because of the physical constraints of manual work. People can walk a lot of dogs, but there are physical limits. Successful investing can be hyperproductive because investing a little or a lot—given a similar level of speed and quality—requires roughly the same amount of knowledge work. For example, Buffett's firm, Berkshire Hathaway, earned more than $20 billion of operating income in 2007 with a staff of less than 20 people. No matter how strong your arms are, this is not possible walking dogs.

Manual work and knowledge work both try to generate surpluses, but each does this differently due to the nature of the work.

Manual Work Productivity	Knowledge Work Productivity
Work is visible	Work is invisible
Work is specialized	Work is holistic
Work is stable	Work is changing
Emphasizes running things	Emphasizes changing things
More structure with fewer decisions	Less structure with more decisions
Focus on the right answers	Focus on the right questions

The three most important differences between manual and knowledge work are:

- Manual work is visible whereas knowledge work is invisible

- Manual work is specialized while knowledge work is holistic

- Manual work is stable but knowledge work is constantly changing

Manual work requires physical tools, whereas knowledge work requires mental models. Mental models—the basis for how we make many of our decisions—are important with knowledge work because *making and implementing decisions* are its basic ingredients.

Given these differences, the role of acceleration is to knowledge work what quality control is to manual work because knowledge work changes so rapidly. With knowledge work, acceleration doesn't imply that the efforts are shoddy or sloppy. Rather, it means that work needs to be applied in real time. It requires ongoing prototyping in the field versus striving for perfection in the office. In the Knowledge Age, what matters most is not what you know but how fast you can apply it. In a rapidly changing competitive environment, acceleration is an essential ingredient in achieving high quality and sustainable competitive advantage.

Factoring in the difference between information and knowledge

Sociologist Daniel Bell was the first person to identify the structural changes leading to the Information Age in the early 1970s [52]. He was careful to make a distinction between information and knowledge. People often get knowledge and information confused and it can impair productivity. This is one reason why information technology has failed so far to significantly or sustainably improve knowledge work productivity. An important difference between the two is that knowledge is alive whereas information is not. As soon as knowledge becomes information, it is no longer knowledge.

It's helpful to think about information versus knowledge in the same way that you think about a mounted deer versus the living deer that it used to be. Even though a deer that has gone through a taxidermy process does resemble a living deer, it cannot function as one. It can no longer respond to change. Neither can information.

Information systems are excellent for manual work productivity because manual work is specialized, stable, and repeatable. With the invisible, holistic, and continually changing nature of knowledge work, data and packaged information unfortunately can't be the productivity driver. It is an important part of the mix, but it is not the driver. Drucker also highlighted this distinction between information and knowledge well when he described something in a book as information and something in practice as knowledge [2].

Reinventing Enterprises using a knowledge work productivity management system

Current wisdom for why Enterprises struggle with knowledge work productivity is that it takes too much up-front investment and is too hard and that knowledge workers just like to be left alone [6]. Drucker believed that a process is needed to turn its potential into performance [1], which requires a knowledge work productivity management system. This is not as simple as handling manual work one way and knowledge work another. These two types of work are part of a larger picture and need to be managed as part of a larger system. A manufacturing company will have a greater manual versus knowledge work percentage than a research lab, but they both require better knowledge work productivity.

Drucker described workers who were both knowledge workers and manual workers as knowledge technologists [3] and correctly saw that these workers would be the fastest growing part of the workforce. Knowledge technologists are a large and growing part of most Enterprises and the knowledge work productivity management system needs to accommodate and capitalize on this at the individual, functional, and organizational levels.

Companies need a better Enterprise system for knowledge work productivity management. This was Drucker's call to action. He did his part, now we must do ours. Since knowledge has become the most important factor of production for many Enterprises and since the half life of knowledge continues to get shorter, it is critical for knowledge workers to systematically learn faster, interact better, and produce better and more accelerated results. We need a different management system. This system, the subject of the next chapter, must be able to help individuals, groups, and organizations manage work that is invisible, holistic, and constantly changing [53] to produce tangible and sustainable surpluses.

Chapter Two: Building the Knowledge Work Productivity Management System

"To manage knowledge work more productively, the underlying system—both the framework and the process—requires a minor amount of initial complexity at the front end to avoid an unworkable amount of complication later on. This difference between complexity and complication is more than semantic. Grandmasters in chess, for example, are successful because they apply a certain amount of cognitive complexity up front. By doing this they can view large chunks of the chessboard, whereas amateurs see a mass of individual pieces. In practice, this makes the game much more complicated for less skilled players and makes novices less successful when they play."

Chapter Two

BUILDING THE KNOWLEDGE WORK PRODUCTIVITY MANAGEMENT SYSTEM

The need for a knowledge work productivity management system was identified by Drucker, but in his role he stopped short of providing the details on how to design it. The lack of such a system has been a problem in Enterprises for decades, especially as companies get larger and more complicated.

With manual work, the underlying business system is visible. A farming friend in college once explained, at the highest level and in the most simple terms, the underlying system for dairy farming. You feed the cows so the cows can produce milk, and then you sell the milk so that you can keep feeding the cows. With this system it's clear if the cows have been fed or not, if the cows have been milked or not, and if the milk has been sold or not.

In most large companies, unlike the farm, knowledge work is less visible and is difficult to manage because it resides in people's heads, and there is no underlying system to channel it. We need to be able to manage the invisible, holistic, and ever-changing nature of these efforts in the same way that farmers are able to manage the visible nature of theirs.

An important characteristic of a system is that it is a whole with interdependent parts and improving one piece doesn't necessarily improve the whole unless it is a constraint. In a company, if marketing is not the constraint, investing more money in marketing will not improve the firm's overall performance. It will actually weaken it by misallocating resources.

A system to manage knowledge work requires both a shared framework and an explicit process. First, a shared framework (i.e., a shared mental model) is needed to get everyone on the same page. Then, in conjunction with this shared framework, a standard process is required to help people manage their knowledge work more productively and sustainably.

To illustrate the implications of this, I'll give an example from a business meeting when I was on the Board of Directors of Coca-Cola Nordic Beverages. There was nothing unusual or confidential about this meeting, otherwise I wouldn't disclose it. But, an example will help shed some light on the nature of knowledge work and illustrate important underlying considerations for making this type of work more productive.

Coca-Cola Nordic Beverages was a joint venture between Carlsberg and The Coca-Cola Company, headquartered in Copenhagen, Denmark. During one meeting we discussed whether to proceed with a large multinational technology project. The Board included the CEO, COO, and CFO of Carlsberg, the president of The Coca-Cola Company's Greater Europe Group, and me.

The project we discussed was an important one for the company. One of the Board members was rightly focused on asking *What* the project was going to achieve. Another member concentrated on *Who* was going to be responsible for what. A third member focused on *How* the project was going to be done. And, for a couple of hours, the company's CEO and CIO fielded a series of questions and follow-up questions and listened to a few personal philosophies and life experiences along the way.

Toward the end of the meeting Bill Casey, who oversaw The Coca-Cola Company's business across seventeen time zones at that time joined the conversation. He shared with the group that 70% of Enterprise Technology projects failed to meet their original objectives and that the average cost overrun was more than 80%. Bill also emphasized that this usually wasn't because of the technology but was most often due to non-technical factors. With this opening, he asked the company's CEO to take a couple of minutes to articulate from a corporate view *Where* he wanted the project to go and *Why*, *What* the project needed to achieve by *When*, *How* those things could best be done, and *Who* needed to be responsible for which tasks.

Not having had a chance to give a lot of thought to the answer, it was—not surprisingly—challenging for the CEO to articulate this off the top of his head. And, it was even more difficult for the Board to jointly agree. From a knowledge work productivity perspective, this was predictable. It's rare in important meetings for people to jointly be clear on the Where, Why, What, When, How and Who questions. This occurs with such regularity that people usually don't even think about it as a knowledge work productivity breakdown. But, that's exactly what it is.

For knowledge work to be managed more productively, as Drucker pointed out, an underlying system is needed. It must get everyone on the same page and properly sequence and accelerate Where-Why-What-When-How-Who. People often *are* clear on many of these things at an individual level. But, collectively, knowledge workers usually have different individual views that don't add up to a shared Enterprise picture. In companies and large Enterprise projects, this results in unproductive work and high failure rates.

To manage knowledge work better, a system with a shared framework and an explicit process is needed. The first step is to determine the right framework and process, which requires the following areas to be thought about and synthesized:

- Initial considerations for the knowledge work system

- Architecture theory base

- Part One: The Framework

- Part Two: The Process

- Using the knowledge work productivity system

- Applying the knowledge work productivity system in practice

Initial considerations for the knowledge work system

Peter Drucker wrote that knowledge work needs to be systematized [3] to improve productivity [17, 18]. Manual work productivity, similar to the dairy farm example, can be managed using the *objective* approaches developed by Frederick Taylor. Knowledge work productivity, on the other hand, requires a combination of subjectivity *and* objectivity.

Using a purely objective approach to manage the fluid and invisible nature of knowledge work has not worked well in practice. When knowledge work is managed like manual work, it tends to get over-engineered, with overly complex governance structures and project designs. Over-engineering work that is invisible, holistic, and ever-changing makes the work take longer and cost more to implement and manage. This explains some of the productivity paradox.

Knowledge work productivity often benefits from a "just in time" mindset versus the "just in case" approach that commonly works so well with manual work. With manual work, taking more time to prepare often improves results and reduces risk because the work is stable and won't change while you're preparing. With the ever-changing nature of knowledge work, "just in time" is typically more productive and less risky. It often benefits from a prototyping mindset.

Prototyping in the field to get work implemented in practice and then making improvements in real time as situations change is often more productive. Knowledge work requires objectivity and subjectivity and an Enterprise ability to discuss, decide upon, implement, and refine decisions better and faster—especially across functions and divisions. Where a good manual work productivity system benefits from being very specialized and mechanized, an effective Enterprise knowledge work productivity system requires a more holistic and better socialized approach [53].

The knowledge work productivity management system—the framework and the process—requires a minor amount of initial complexity at the front end to avoid an unworkable amount of complication [54] later on. This difference between complexity and complication is more than semantic. Grandmasters in chess, for example, are successful because they apply a certain amount of cognitive complexity up front. By doing this they can view large chunks of the chessboard, whereas amateurs see a mass of individual pieces. In practice, this makes the game much more complicated for less skilled players and makes novices less successful when they play [55].

A key difference between complexity and complication is that complexity has a coherent architecture [56-58] and can be effectively managed. In contrast, complication is largely random and therefore becomes unmanageable over time [54]. Large Enterprises and large Enterprise projects regularly struggle, not because they are too complex, but because they are too complicated.

To illustrate, consider the beverage business. In this industry large soft drink companies are relatively simple from a complexity perspective. They market, sell, merchandise, distribute, and manufacture packaged and fountain beverages. While this work isn't complex, the soft drink business is actually very complicated. The interactions within and between family bottlers, independent bottlers, publicly-traded bottlers, company bottlers, brand owners, a large and diverse customer base, and a variety of other important parties and personalities make the industry difficult to manage and change. This will be revisited In Chapter Ten.

To manage knowledge work, as with the game of chess, it is useful to introduce a minor amount of complexity—a coherent architecture through a shared framework and process—on the front end to eliminate unmanageable complications later. Similar to any good model, it needs to simplify while also being robust enough so that knowledge work tasks can productively self-organize around the architecture in a variety of situations and under various conditions. To build the system that Drucker suggested, a high-level architecture is required, with a shared framework and a repeatable process. The social sciences provide the raw materials to do this successfully.

Architecture theory base

For individuals, functions, and organizations to improve their Enterprises on a sustainable basis [3, 59], a shared framework is required [33]. Without a shared management architecture, given the invisible and ever-changing nature of knowledge work, employees will struggle with various invisible and conflicting mental models [7].

Being able to develop a practical yet research-supported management system for knowledge work benefited greatly from the social sciences. One risk of describing its lineage in this section is that there will be some who believe it is too academic and others who will believe it is not pure enough from an academic standpoint. Since the rest of this book is more business oriented in nature, if the academic lineage of the knowledge work productivity system is not important to you, you may want to spend less time going through this section. Otherwise, I suggest a thorough examination. Whatever your choice, it is written in a style that should suit both practicing and academic business thinkers.

The work of two professors, Gibson Burrell and Gareth Morgan, was especially important to build the knowledge work productivity system used in this book. Thirty years ago, when they were faculty members of England's Lancaster University, Burrell and Morgan published an important book on the history of sociological paradigms, classifying a comprehensive set of them into four groups using the four poles of subjectivity, objectivity, stability, and change [60]. Using more business-oriented language, their classification of sociological paradigms had four primary orientations:

- Envisioning-Intuition

- Designing-Analysis

- Building-Process

- Operating-Emotional

Burrell and Morgan labeled these four orientations Interpretive, Functionalist, Radical Structuralist, and Radical Humanist. In the knowledge work productivity management system, they are labeled Envision, Design, Build and Operate.

The Burrell and Morgan framework was groundbreaking for its intended purpose to categorize a large number of sociological paradigms. A side benefit is that in business it also provides an excellent working model for understanding and improving knowledge work productivity. I have seen it work thousands of times as an underlying architecture to help business people make the invisible nature of knowledge work more visible and more productive.

It is not surprising that a working knowledge work productivity framework comes from the social sciences. Enterprises are social constructions [9, 31, 61-64], knowledge work is a highly sociological exercise, and Drucker himself considered management a social institution [65]. Even though there has not been a single model to integrate the social sciences [66], there are commonalities between sociological models that support using Burrell and Morgan's framework as the basis for helping individuals, functions, and organizations manage knowledge work productivity better.

Four-quadrant models—such as Envision-Design-Build-Operate—are frequently used in business *and* in the social sciences. But, there is commonly a difference in how they are constructed. In the highly objective world of most business people [21], practitioners often compare two variables to create four quadrant models. For example, the Boston Consulting Group's famous "2 x 2" matrix creates four quadrants by comparing business growth and market share. This results in the four quadrants of high share/high growth, high share/low growth, low share/high growth, and low share/low growth.

An important difference between 2 x 2 matrices used in business and many four quadrant models in the social sciences is that social science models are more likely to compare and contrast two sets of opposites [44, 60] instead of two variables. Comparing and contrasting two sets of opposites produces four variables that are not mutually exclusive. Often they are of a yin and yang variety. This results in much more holistic frameworks. For example, the Burrell and Morgan model doesn't compare stability versus change or objectivity versus subjectivity. It compares both at the same time and accommodates every possible variation in between.

Using a model that embraces opposites from the social sciences is useful when applied to knowledge work productivity because Enterprises are complex, holistic, and ever-changing and have many opposing forces at work. In business, integrating opposites occurs regularly. For example, an objective approach works well in accounting, whereas a subjective approach often works better in sales. The approach is not inherently good or bad. The most productive approach generally depends upon the situation.

Carl Jung [67], the Swiss psychiatrist who inspired the popular *Myers-Briggs Type Indicator®* [68], also embraced opposites. For example, two opposites that he focused on were thinking versus feeling. He also recognized the dominant and secondary orientations of these types of opposing characteristics depending on the situation and referred to them as the General and Lieutenant. Both are needed, he suggested, but one works in the background while the other is in command at any point in time. Business practitioner Ned Hermann [69, 70], creator of the *Herrmann Brain Dominance Instrument®*, also saw this when he worked at General Electric. Similar to Jung, he observed that different orientations were less *or* more effective in different situations.

There are many examples of the benefits of embracing opposites in the social sciences [9, 44, 67, 71-75]. When these are examined through a business lens, four opposites—related to knowledge work productivity—are particularly useful. They are, consistent with Drucker, objectivity, subjectivity, knowledge, and work. These poles produce a knowledge work framework with four orientations:

- Subjective knowledge

- Objective knowledge

- Objective work

- Subjective work

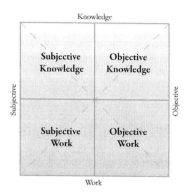

This works well in practice and defines the knowledge work productivity management system used in this book. It is consistent with Drucker's insight that we must live and work in two worlds: the world of ideas and knowledge and the world of people and work [1]. From a social science perspective, this framework also relates well to the four Burrell and Morgan sociological paradigm orientations (intuition-analysis-process-emotional). Tying this all together and using common business language, the resulting four primary knowledge work-behavior areas are:

- Envision—subjective knowledge

- Design—objective knowledge

- Build—objective work

- Operate—subjective work

Relating this architecture to the Board of Directors example at the beginning of the chapter, ENVISION is needed to focus on Where you intend to go and Why. DESIGN is necessary to concentrate on What you need to do and When. BUILD is needed to focus on How to best implement the design. OPERATE is required to concentrate on Who needs to be responsible for which tasks. Managed in a holistic way and in the right order, these four steps are essential to improve knowledge work productivity and reinvent Enterprises.

Part One: The Framework

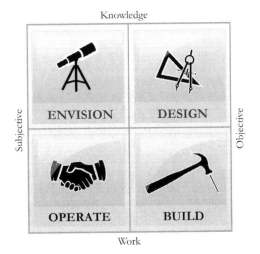

Drucker wrote that economic results are human achievements [34]. They are neither purely qualitative nor completely quantitative. Similarly, since most employees are knowledge technologists, knowledge work cannot be completely separated from manual work. A good knowledge work productivity framework must be able to help individuals, functions, and organizations productively and continually manage the opposing forces of knowledge, work, subjectivity, and objectivity. It must accommodate the fact that almost all work has manual and knowledge components.

One way to visualize the knowledge work framework described in this book is to think of it as a map with a North Pole, South Pole, West Coast and East Coast. The North Pole is *Knowledge*—a mental output. The South Pole is *Work*—a physical output. The West Coast is *Subjectivity*—an intuitive output. The East Coast is *Objectivity*—a structured output. These opposing sets of poles produce the following four knowledge work productivity work-behavior areas.

ENVISION—Subjective Knowledge

The Northwest—Subjective Knowledge—orientation produces the Envision work-behavior area. Influenced by the external environment and the firm's long term destination, it asks and answers the question *Where do we intend to go and Why?*

- In companies this quadrant includes qualitative knowledge functions such as research and development, strategy, marketing, and other externally focused functions including public affairs and legal.

- The *strength* of highly Envision-oriented people and functions is an ability to think outside the box. The *weakness* is that they can also be impractical when it comes to what is most important in the short term.

- Attributes of people, functions, and organizations with an Envision orientation include:

  - Thinking strategically
  - Setting a visionary destination
  - Thinking inventively
  - Generating imaginative ideas
  - Thinking creatively
  - Pioneering new ideas
  - Brainstorming new ideas

DESIGN—*Objective Knowledge*

The Northeast—Objective Knowledge—orientation produces the Design work-behavior area. Connected to the Envision quadrant, it asks and answers the question *What do we need to do and When?*

- In companies this quantitative knowledge quadrant produces the business logic of the Enterprise. It includes functions such as finance, accounting, engineering, and planning.

- The *strength* of highly design-oriented people and functions is the ability to turn a vision into a plan and measure progress against that plan. The *weakness* is that they can be intolerant when a changing world conflicts with their pre-established models, plans, and measures.

- Attributes of people, functions, and organizations with the Design orientation include:

  - Analyzing situations
  - Defining clear policies
  - Defining detailed objectives
  - Planning budgets
  - Establishing clear performance measures
  - Judging performance objectively
  - Making decisions by the numbers

BUILD—*Objective Work*

The Southeast—Objective Work—orientation produces the Build work-behavior area. Connected to the Design quadrant, it asks and answers the question *How can the work best get done?*

- In companies, this objective hands-on orientation produces the systems, processes, and infrastructure for the Enterprise. It includes functions such as manufacturing, information systems, and logistics.

- The *strength* of highly Build-oriented people and functions is that they are practical, precise, and good at turning a plan into something tangible. The *weakness* is that they can lack vision when new systems and processes are needed for new times.

- Attributes of people, functions, and organizations with the Build orientation include implementing:

  –Standard processes
  –Step-by-step procedures
  –Important projects
  –Integrated programs
  –Proven methods
  –Practical solutions
  –Roles and responsibilities

OPERATE

OPERATE—*Subjective Work*

The Southwest—Subjective Work—orientation produces the Operate work-behavior area. Connected to the Build quadrant, it asks and answers the question *Who is responsible for which tasks?*

- In companies this qualitative hands-on orientation creates and maintains the key personal relationships for the Enterprise. It includes functions such as sales, coaching, and communications.

- The *strength* of highly Operate-oriented people and functions is that they are great at opportunistically thriving in a changing world using personal relationships. The *weakness* is that it can be difficult for them to conform to pre-determined Enterprise plans and standard processes.

- Attributes of people, functions, and organizations with the Operate orientation include:

  –Building personal relationships
  –Working in teams
  –Coaching others
  –Supporting others
  –Relating to people
  –Communicating
  –Changing spontaneously

Part Two: The Process

The knowledge work productivity and Enterprise reinvention system requires both a framework and a process. The first part of the system is the Envision-Design-Build-Operate framework just described. It is needed to make it possible for people to share the same mental model. The second part of the system is its steering process. A repeatable steering mechanism is needed to help knowledge workers productively sequence their work on a sustainable basis. The framework is based on the Burrell and Morgan sociological paradigms model and the steering process benefits from the science of cybernetics.

Cybernetics is the science of relationships, control, and organization [55]. It was first used by mathematician Norbert Wiener [76] in 1948 to facilitate self-steering. For instance, this is how radar is used to help steer airplanes. By using new information generated by radar, a plane's flight path can be automatically adjusted to stay on course. Similar to productive knowledge work, cybernetics requires a goal and a statement of how to achieve it [55].

Sociologist Talcott Parsons applied Wiener's work on cybernetics to social systems in 1951 [9, 77] through his General Theory of Action [75, 78, 79]. Parsons established what he termed the "cybernetic hierarchy." This was designed to give an order to organizational actions, based on the control that organizations have and the information they receive. This cybernetic hierarchy—from a control perspective—is logically consistent with the Envision-Design-Build-Operate knowledge work productivity framework. For example, in the Theory of Action, *Envision* adapts to the external environment. This action leads to the goals that are *Designed*. This leads to *Building* an integrated Enterprise. This must support and motivate the *Operators* to ultimately succeed.

Managers need to integrate the cybernetic process into the knowledge work productivity framework to produce a working management system. By following and ensuring that individuals-functions-organizations follow the cybernetic hierarchy, managers can use Envision-Design-Build-Operate as a repeatable management process to improve productivity on a sustainable basis.

The knowledge work productivity management system works well in practice because it is both a framework and a process. The framework helps people benefit from a shared mental model to define the work. The cybernetic process then provides a systematic way for individuals, functions, and organizations to productively manage the work [80, 81].

Using the knowledge work productivity system

Having personally applied the knowledge work productivity system thousands of times, it is clear that the two root causes of unproductive knowledge work are when there are gaps in the four work-behavior areas or when the cybernetic process gets out of sequence.

One of the keys to accelerating Envision-Design-Build-Operate is to manage them as a unit so that when one part of the system changes the rest of the system can adjust productively. All four parts of the knowledge work productivity system are important in and of themselves. They need to be made more productive as part of an entire system. Knowledge work gets stuck when the four parts of the system become disconnected or out of sequence. This is true for large Enterprises, large projects, and large government programs as well.

For example, when Social Security began, Envision-Design-Build-Operate were linked. Most people lived to be about 65, and the nation was able to support the relatively few people who were fortunate enough to live longer lives. Where-Why-What-When-How-Who were connected and the system was sustainable. More than seventy years later, Americans live almost fifteen years longer, but the system hasn't adapted. Envision-Design-Build-Operate have become increasingly disconnected over the decades to the point where now, with no easy solution, the nation will be required to pay a heavy price.

Enterprises don't need to suffer this way if they continually reinvent themselves. In the ever-changing competitive environment, the Envision-Design-Build-Operate knowledge work productivity management system is a stable platform for continuous adaptation. Enterprises can enter the proverbial river at the same spot, even though they are truly never entering the same river twice. In the words of the late singer-songwriter John Denver, our Enterprises can continually "come home to a place we've never been before [82]." In the metaphorical river of business, the knowledge work productivity system can simultaneously help to anchor us and move us faster.

Applying the knowledge work productivity system in practice

In the late 1990s I was interviewed for Microsoft co-founder Bill Gates' book, *Business at the Speed of Thought* [83]. In his book, Gates emphasizes that the past was about reengineering but the future depends on velocity. With knowledge work, velocity is at the heart of the productivity opportunity.

Sustainable success is not simply driven by urgency, because you can urgently go in the wrong direction. Knowledge work productivity is not about speed *or* direction. Similar to velocity, it is a function of speed *and* direction. By applying the knowledge work productivity system, Enterprises can increase their velocity—their change divided by time.

Consistent with the Enterprise velocity equation, Peter Drucker wrote that the three dimensions of an economic task were to make the present business effective, identify and realize its potential, and make it into a different business for a different future [34]. In our rapidly changing global economy, this needs to be accelerated. The four-part knowledge work productivity mantra based on the social sciences and cybernetics is:

- *Where* do we intend to go and *Why?*

- *What* needs to happen *When?*

- *How* can those things best get done?

- *Who* is going to be responsible for which tasks?

The knowledge work productivity management system is to Enterprises what competition is to capitalism. It breathes life into it, creates order out of chaos, and improves Enterprise velocity. Drucker wrote that doing this was essential to economic tasks [34]. It is also essential to Enterprise reinvention and our long term economic prosperity. The Envision step, which is the subject of the next chapter, is where it all begins.

Chapter Three: Step One of the Knowledge Work Productivity System—ENVISION

"When I hear of two-pronged strategies, I can't help but think of the somewhat famous freaks of nature: Ditto the pig and Thelma and Louise. Ditto was a pig born with two mouths and two snouts. Sadly, Ditto died from inhaling food into one snout while the other snout was eating. Thelma and Louise was a two-headed corn snake at the San Diego Zoo. Two-headed snakes can't survive in an unprotected environment because they fight with one another over food, have trouble deciding on which way to go, and can't respond quickly to an attack. This is similar to how Enterprises act when they don't have a clear and unified strategy."

Chapter Three

STEP ONE OF THE KNOWLEDGE WORK PRODUCTIVITY SYSTEM—ENVISION

With knowledge work productivity and Enterprise reinvention, if you *don't* know where you are going, any road will get you there. If you *do* know, great things are possible. The Envision step is important to establish your destination. It is the starting point to help you clearly articulate your intent and purpose so that your destination can be productively achieved. Envision asks and answers the key question: *Where do we intend to go and Why?*

This needs to integrate important external factors including: who is our customer? What challenges are they facing? How can we help them lower their costs and be more successful? It clarifies what your business is and what it should be.

To be most productive, the Envision work-behavior area must keep the Enterprise at least one step ahead of the problems that the organization faces—always focusing on becoming better.

When there is not a clear Enterprise vision, a number of dysfunctions will develop. They include people working hard without making much progress, difficulties that result from inconsistent and incompatible goals within and across functions, duplication of effort, and critical projects that never get started or do get started but are delayed or never finished.

One way to visualize the Envision-Design-Build-Operate work-behavior areas in the knowledge work productivity system is to relate them to a map of the United States. Following the cybernetic process, it's like having a brainstorming session in Seattle (Envision), crunching numbers in Boston (Design), developing infrastructure in Miami (Build), and cultivating relationships in Los Angeles (Operate). Using this metaphor, Seattle (Envision) is the first leg of the journey.

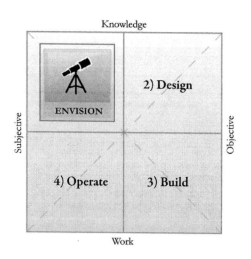

Step One: Envision

The Envision step—focused on Where your Enterprise intends to go and Why—is vital for adaptation. It is needed to help you and your company visualize, in a changing environment, a future that is different from the present and the past. It is also required to make strategic tradeoffs at the Enterprise level. Productive visions, made possible by excellent subjective knowledge orientations, help Enterprises transcend their historic practices and organizational boundaries with greater effectiveness and efficiency. They are the necessary catalyst to help individuals, functions, and organizations reach new destinations in a changing world.

Productive visions are positive and also push people out of their comfort zones. This requires establishing a clear tension between the present and the future—simultaneously ensuring constancy of purpose and instilling a fear of the status quo that is greater than the fear of the unknown. Productive visions need to connect the dots between Where the Enterprise has been, Where it is, Where it needs to go, and Why.

It's important that Envision, as the first step of the knowledge work productivity system, be connected to the Design, Build, and Operate work-behavior areas, be productive, and be sustainable. Entrepreneurs such as Sam Walton of Walmart [84] and Ray Kroc of McDonald's [85] were very successful at doing this. They were masters at integrating their vision, plan, structure, and people and then scaling the entire system over time.

A productive vision is not the same as a good idea. It requires that the idea be made operational by testing, scaling, and continually improving it in the marketplace. It separates the creative dreamers from the successful implementers. For Enterprises to develop and properly manage productive visions through the Envision step, several areas are important to understand and synthesize:

- Ensuring that your vision clarifies Where you intend to go and Why

- Using your vision to accelerate Enterprise tradeoffs

- Accelerating tradeoffs to improve your customer value and innovation

- Using customer value and innovation to focus your Enterprise strategy

- Reconstructing your strategy into a sustainable competitive advantage

Ensuring that your vision clarifies Where you intend to go and Why

Productive visions predict the future by inventing it—with leadership, clarity, and constancy of purpose. They integrate an honest respect for history, discontent with the present, and develop a clear long term destination. This paves the way for a winning game plan that capitalizes on the Enterprise's unique collection of assets—including its operational capabilities, customer relationships, and executive team—to improve corporate performance faster and more sustainably.

Determining what it will take to win is an important part of a productive Enterprise vision—not focusing on where the fish are but on where they are going. It needs to create a sense of urgency while simultaneously setting a target that is clear and stable over time [86]. Productive visions establish a formal mechanism for individuals-functions-organizations to create a sense of certainty in an uncertain world through a future oriented view and language around Where the Enterprise intends to go and Why. This then can help Enterprises more productively direct their own destiny and self-correct when they are going off course.

Constancy of purpose [87, 88] is an important success factor because each step of the Envision-Design-Build-Operate system takes longer than the one before it. Design takes longer than Envision, Build takes longer than Design, and Operate takes longer than Build. Yet, this cycle needs to be completed for knowledge work to be productive and for Enterprises to be reinvented. Every time the Envision-Design-Build-Operate cycle is interrupted, it reduces productivity and creates the equivalent of knowledge work scrap.

For instance, if an executive changes Envision (i.e., Where the Enterprise intends to go and Why) while the organization is still working on the previous destination, much of the work that was done on the previous vision will lose its value. This type of knowledge work waste is very common when management shuffling produces changes in direction, when the same leaders keep changing their minds, or when there is no constancy of purpose. Since knowledge work is invisible, much of this waste is never noticed. It is costly nevertheless.

For knowledge work to be productive, the Envision work-behavior area needs to establish the vision, keep it consistent, and ensure that there is constant tension between Where the Enterprise is now and Where it intends to go. To properly manage this tension, it helps when people in the Enterprise know Why the change is intended and if they are dissatisfied and even afraid of the status quo. When discomfort is created, comfort can then be provided through a positive vision, linked to a clear plan [88]. This plan is an important part of the Design step, which focuses on what's important now and is the subject of the next chapter. For Envision to be productive, the blend of a positive vision with fear of the status quo needs to be more compelling to employees than the personal costs required to change [89].

Productive visions need to first disrupt order to create it [61]. This requires the tension noted previously. It also requires consistency over time so that Enterprises can, with constancy of purpose, progress along the Envision-Design-Build-Operate continuum. When this is achieved, executive teams can accelerate their tradeoff decisions and improve Enterprise performance on a sustainable basis.

Using your vision to accelerate Enterprise tradeoffs

Knowledge work productivity improvements will only be sustainable if you've clearly established your destination [26]. Once your Enterprise vision is clear, necessary organizational tradeoffs can be implemented and accelerated, including those related to surfacing and solving operational bottlenecks, improving the productivity of your customer relationships, decreasing unproductive assets, and reducing unproductive operating expenses.

A clear vision is required to accelerate Enterprise tradeoffs between organizational levels and across functions because it makes the productive and unproductive work more *visible*. Without it, employees will be working with conflicting information, incompatible objectives, and inconsistent definitions for success. When people, functions, and organizations don't share the same view of success, they will not be able to act as a single force. A clearly established and shared vision is very important [90] to manage scarce corporate resources—human, capital, and technological—for better and faster results.

There is an old saying that a tree cannot prune itself. In large Enterprises, for the new to grow, the old often needs to be pruned or even abandoned. In practice, this requires a clear vision combined with a top-down Enterprise governance structure. Bottom-up feedback is important, but this is quite different from attempting to achieve bottom-up decision making through an over-engineered governance structure. To accelerate tradeoffs, Enterprises need to establish a clear destination and have an accelerated tradeoff capability in place. Then, they will be well positioned to connect the dots between:

- Envision—Where you intend to go and Why

- Design—What needs to be done and When

- Build—How those things can best be done

- Operate—Who is responsible for which tasks

Tradeoff decisions cannot be delegated. The fact that over-engineered governance structures are often put in place to try to do this is a key reason why Enterprise change projects struggle so often. Many things can and should be delegated, but not tradeoff decisions. Productive tradeoffs require that the decision maker be in every meeting that requires his or her decision. Somewhat counter-intuitively, over time, this will actually reduce the number of meetings required for decision makers. It will *greatly* reduce the number of meetings required for non-decision makers.

To accelerate Enterprise tradeoff decisions, the use of consensus needs to be rethought. Input is critical, but consensus is too often impractical and unproductive when tradeoffs are required. Even with two people consensus can be difficult. With ten it's impossible. Yet, many large Enterprises continue to cherish the idea. A steering committee of peers is not a substitute for Enterprise decision making.

Meetings that don't have the ultimate decision maker present have no choice but to depend upon consensus. As a result, they have built-in knowledge work productivity barriers. They become the Anaconda snake of large Enterprises and large Enterprise projects. The Anaconda doesn't bite. It kills its prey through suffocation. It's easy to get suffocated by meetings that don't result in a decision or an action. They are incapable of producing decisions that benefit one function while disadvantaging another and this stops Enterprise progress by creating knowledge work gridlocks. Unfortunately, these middle management gridlocks are often invisible to the ultimate decision makers and fester unproductively for long periods of time.

Even though consensus is impractical, bottom-up input is critical for good Enterprise decision making. It's important that a holistic cross-section of people give input so that Enterprises can benefit from the best thinking and knowledge. However, inputs are different from decisions. In large Enterprises it is important to explicitly identify those who have the right to make a decision versus those who *only* have the right to make a comment or suggestion or point out the risks. As part of this process, when meetings systematically include the ultimate decision maker, Enterprise knowledge work will immediately become more productive.

There will be mistakes made using this approach, just as mistakes are made when governance structures are over-engineered. When there are errors using an accelerated Enterprise decision-making process, these problems can be corrected faster and better through the same decision makers. Perfection exists only in the dictionary. Rapidly changing global environments require clear Enterprise visions and an accelerated Enterprise decision-making process with a spirit of action, imperfection, forgiveness, and continuous improvement. It is far better to do important things imperfectly than nothing flawlessly.

Accelerating tradeoffs to improve your customer value and innovation

Tradeoffs need to be judged on the Enterprise value they create. Value is generated by the customer needs being served, the profit associated with serving those needs, and the sustainable growth rate of the Enterprise providing the applicable products and services. From a customer value and innovation standpoint, focus produces superiority, superiority increases scarcity, and scarcity allows companies to better manage the balance between pricing power and customer value [13].

Enterprises need to produce value *with* their customers to become more valuable themselves. Drucker went so far as to say that the purpose of a business is to create a customer [34, 91]. Because of the fragmented nature of many organizations, it's easy for companies to lose their customer focus. But this focus is critical, and it's important to concentrate on creating value *with* customers—versus purely *for* customers—so that value can be both created and shared equitably.

Enterprises produce value and innovate successfully with customers in two ways. They lower their customer's costs and they improve their performance [92]. The best companies do this better. If Enterprises can't lower customer costs or improve their performance, they have no sustainable value proposition. Companies will know they have lost their competitive advantage with customers when they lose their pricing power and find it difficult to grow profitably.

Productive firms need to focus their efforts [34] and accelerate tradeoffs [93] with customers to improve Enterprise value on a sustainable basis. As Drucker pointed out, companies can either concentrate their knowledge and diversify products or concentrate products and diversify knowledge [34]. As the market changes, this may require killing off or spinning off something that has made your company great [94]. While difficult, organized abandonment [5] is important because it is the most productive way to reallocate resources and compete successfully with new competitors [35] in a changing world.

As part of your customer value proposition, innovation must grow profits to qualify as successful innovation. If a company's innovation doesn't result in commercial success, it's not productive. In this light, Drucker wrote that innovation is the only thing that earns a genuine profit [35] and that it shouldn't be confused with novelty. Grafting innovation onto an established company has also proven not to work [5]. The test for productive innovation is not whether you, your boss, or the board like or dislike something, but whether customers embrace it enough to pay a good price for it [95] and keep buying more of it.

With innovation, many companies have learned the hard lesson that it is inevitably more profitable to take advantage of a new trend than to fight it [34]. In the technology area, IBM lost the PC profit pool to Microsoft. IBM considered itself a hardware company in the 1970s when Microsoft emerged and saw the PC as a software opportunity. More than thirty years later Microsoft has so far lost much of the Web opportunity to Google. Microsoft viewed the Web through a desktop software lens, and Google saw the potential value of connecting browser-based Internet searches, eyeballs, and advertising.

For innovation to be productive, Drucker stressed that it needs to change the wealth-producing potential of existing resources, without trying to graft the innovation onto the base business. A good example of doing this successfully was when Pacific Telesis launched AirTouch Communications. AirTouch was a large public stock offering in the mid-1990s that later turned into Verizon Wireless.

I had the opportunity to study AirTouch and Pacific Telesis during that time and was able to interview AirTouch CEO Sam Ginn and Pacific Telesis CEO Phil Quigley in San Francisco and Stanford, California. When Ginn was CEO of Pacific Telesis, prior to Quigley, he incubated AirTouch. Incubating it within a company whose family tree began as the Ma Bell monopoly was a remarkable achievement. Sam Ginn later became CEO of AirTouch when it was spun off, and he and his team created substantial value for consumers, employees, and shareholders during their time there.

Even though AirTouch was able to incubate inside a company with plenty of resources, this is not what made it successful. Most start-ups within companies do not ultimately perform well because they are cultural misfits and can't compete effectively for resources as they grow. With AirTouch, it was critically important to have the group's counter-cultural behaviors protected from the rest of the company by Ginn. It was even more important for AirTouch to eventually be able to come of age and spread its wings as a stand-alone public company outside of the more established Pacific Telesis that incubated it.

As was the case with AirTouch, productive innovation needs to combine growth and pricing power. Owning your innovation is also important. It reminds me of a Larry King interview I once saw with entertainer Jon Bon Jovi. During the interview, Bon Jovi made the comment that if you don't write and perform your own material, the best you can hope for is to be a lounge singer. Excellent businesses can be built by copying the success of others, but truly great businesses envision and then innovate their own path. Compare Apple and Dell in 2008. Both were great success stories for their founders. Nonetheless, Apple consistently had a fraction of Dell's revenue but enjoyed a far greater market value. Apple owned the secret sauce—its operating system and an incredible track record of exquisitely designed and integrated innovations.

Productive innovation is a key driver for profitable growth, focused on doing a few things well. This includes increasing sales to existing customers, developing new customers, creating successful new products and services, consolidating operations, and forming productive alliances [96]. In this context, it is important for customer value, innovation, and accelerated tradeoffs to converge to create a strong customer-oriented value and innovation mindset. By helping customers solve their problems, Enterprises will solve their own [88]. If you want something, give it.

In certain ways building a customer-centered company is like building a church. Dr. Robert H. Schuller, the founder of the Crystal Cathedral in Garden Grove, California, wrote in the 1980s that building a church required answering three questions [97]:

- Would it be a great thing?

- Would it solve someone's problems?

- Is anybody else doing the right job?

These are great questions for every Enterprise. To increase your value, it is important to focus on customers, innovation, and growth. Ask yourself, "What would I do with my company if I had to personally buy it today and then sell it three years from now?" Based on that, what would you do next? What wouldn't you do? Then, think about your company over a twenty-year time horizon. Consider which short term changes also make sense in the long term. When you have a match, you are well positioned to move forward—via the Envision step—made possible by a clear vision, accelerated tradeoffs, your customer focus, and productive innovation.

Using customer value and innovation to focus your Enterprise strategy

During the Envision step it is important to think about your firm's strategy *after* the customer value and innovation [98] thinking has been done. Then, when your strategy is executed, it will benefit from being market driven and result in at least one sustainable competitive advantage [99].

Your Enterprise strategy is an essential part of the Envision step [99-102] because it is the embodiment of Where you intend to go and Why. It sets the pace for sustainable knowledge work productivity and Enterprise reinvention by directing resources effectively and efficiently throughout the entire Envision-Design-Build-Operate knowledge work productivity process [103].

Strategy is not the same thing as planning. It's best when it is *not* highly detailed [104]. It needs to establish at the Enterprise level what the business currently is and articulate what it needs to become and why [34]. It is not a quantitative exercise but is driven by subjective knowledge. It is not the same thing as strategic planning, which is a mixture of the Envision (subjective knowledge) and Design (objective knowledge) work-behavior areas.

The strategy process is commonly unproductive in large Enterprises because it is not holistic enough. Rather than being analytically *driven*, your Enterprise strategy should be analytically *supported*. Beginning with existing customer relationships, capabilities, and feedback, your strategy should begin with clarifying *Where you intend to go and Why*. This will then help focus your company's efforts on What needs to happen and When, How to best do those things, and Who should be responsible for which tasks.

One sign of a productivity problem with corporate strategy is when companies generate a lot of internal ideas that neither get implemented nor stopped. Companies that favor creative ideas over the difficult work of implementing one or two are not visionary. They are schizophrenic. Being inside this type of company feels a little like an Enterprise version of the *Whac-A-Mole* game that I used to watch my children play when they were young at Chuck E. Cheese restaurants. New ideas come popping up rapidly and randomly, and energy is expended on whacking down the distractions rather than on implementing the ideas that have previously been decided upon.

Chief information officers commonly struggle with this problem when different functional managers fall in love with new technologies related to their respective areas of expertise. Over time, if a lot of these systems are adopted, corporate application portfolios begin to resemble Enterprise toy boxes, with a mishmash of applications that local managers couldn't live without at one time or another but are no longer important. Without a clear strategy, as managers move on or as new applications come onto the market, these types of systems often lose their sponsors and become expensive additions to the application orphanage.

As highlighted earlier, a productive Enterprise strategy needs to emerge from socially constructed visions [104, 105] with customers and other key stakeholders. The dialogues should result in a clearly articulated destination through the company's line management [106]. Japanese strategist Keniche Ohmae reinforced this when he emphasized that an inability to clearly articulate a strategy in a single sentence is a clear sign that there is something wrong with the strategy itself. [105] In Hollywood, the same axiom applies to screenplays. Movie producers often say, "Give it to me in one sentence!" If you can't—if it takes you two or three sentences to get the main idea across—they know your script is scattered and not well-plotted. I've always tried to resist the term "strategies" in business for this reason, because I believe that a productive Enterprise strategy is singular not plural.

In addition to the need for clarity, it's important to accept and embrace that every productive strategy will possess clear weaknesses [107]. Every dog has its fleas and every good strategy has its faults. No executable strategy is perfect. The least perfect strategy is one that tries to be all things to all people. Strategy, like customer value creation and innovation, requires focus. You will know that you have a productive strategy when executives can say no to good ideas that are incongruent.

Creating and implementing a productive strategy is hard because it's comforting for people to keep their options open. On a number of occasions I've heard executives talk about two-pronged strategies. When I hear that, I can't help but think of the somewhat famous freaks of nature: Ditto the pig and Thelma and Louise. Ditto was a pig born with two mouths and two snouts. Sadly, Ditto died from inhaling food into one snout while the other snout was eating. Thelma and Louise was a two-headed corn snake at the San Diego Zoo. Two-headed snakes can't survive in an unprotected environment because they fight with one another over food, have trouble deciding on which way to go, and can't respond quickly to an attack. This is similar to how Enterprises act when they don't have a clear strategy.

A variety of useful tools have been developed over the years to help companies formalize and clarify their corporate strategy so they don't suffer the fate of Ditto or Thelma and Louise. They are useful and need to be linked to Envision-Design-Build-Operate to make a sustainable difference in the Knowledge Age. Here are some popular tools:

- Michael Porter's Five Forces [92]. It helps Enterprises focus on rivalry, competitive entry, substitution, buyer power, supplier power, and value chain analysis.

- Stanford Research Institute's original SWOT analysis. It helps companies focus on their Strengths, Weaknesses, Opportunities, and Threats.

- The Boston Consulting Group's Portfolio Matrix. Based on market share and growth, it helps firms analyze and identify "cash cows," "stars," "question marks," and "dogs."

- Various forms of Stakeholder Analysis. These help Enterprises examine strategic groups and individuals and their relationships to the firm.

Regardless of the tools used, creating an Enterprise strategy that begins with your customer-centered value and innovation [108] proposition is critical to the Envision step. Doing this productively will improve your ability to successfully implement your Enterprise strategy in the marketplace and earn at least one sustainable competitive advantage with your customers.

Reconstructing your strategy into a sustainable competitive advantage

Market leadership does not cause competitive advantage. Competitive advantage causes market leadership. Using a sports illustration, the Brazilian soccer player Pelé, one of the greatest scorers of all time, often practiced as a goalie. He learned what was hard to handle defensively and then used that knowledge to his advantage when he played offensively in a real game. He wasn't great because he was Pelé, he was Pelé because he was great. In business, working with your customers to earn and extend competitive advantage is equivalent to practicing as a goalie. The competitive advantage that you develop will then result in market leadership over time. In a changing market you won't be the best because you have a great brand. You will have a great brand because you're the best.

Sustainable competitive advantage will result from your unique set of customers, their specific needs, and your special Enterprise capabilities.

Concentrating on your competitors versus your customers will eventually result in price wars. Working *with* your customers to lower their costs and make them more successful will be your company's most productive path toward sustainable competitive advantage [105, 109]. This will create better product and service differentiation, stronger personal relationships, better intellectual property, better cost structures, and more sustainable switching costs [92].

Turning your Enterprise strategy into at least one sustainable competitive advantage begins with the Envision step. As part of this, you will need to translate your vision into a clear direction that your customers can see, a focused product and service offering that your customers prefer, an efficient operating infrastructure that your customers depend upon, and meaningful human relationships that your customers trust. Your value proposition should be memorable, meaningful, transferable, adaptable, and *protectable* [110]. If everyone can do it, you won't be able to make a lot of money at it [111].

The Envision work-behavior area is the first step toward sustainable competitive advantage. It begins with Where you intend to go and Why. If your company is clear on this, great things are possible. Nonetheless, it is only one part of the four step Enterprise reinvention process. Envision in isolation is not sufficient. It needs to be made more actionable through the Design step, the subject of the next chapter. The Design work-behavior area asks and answers the question, defined by the company's vision, "What do you need to do and When?"

Chapter Four: Step Two of the Knowledge Work Productivity System—DESIGN

"To improve knowledge work productivity and Enterprise reinvention, it is important for planning to adapt holistically as changes occur inside and outside the company. New things will need to be started and certain old things will need to be stopped. In this regard, never put off until tomorrow what you can forget about entirely."

STEP TWO OF THE KNOWLEDGE WORK PRODUCTIVITY SYSTEM—DESIGN

To improve productivity and reinvention on a sustainable basis, once you have established Where your company intends to go and Why in the Envision work-behavior area, it's important to concentrate on *What needs to happen and When* in the Design step. The purpose of the Design step is to convert the Enterprise vision into a productive plan. In companies, the Design work-behavior area includes functions such as finance, accounting, planning, and engineering. Preferred ways to solve problems using objective knowledge orientations include analyzing numbers, budgeting, and judging performance through quantitative measures.

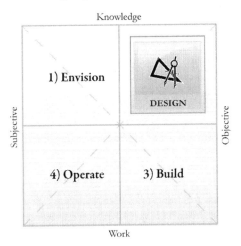

A key strength of Design people and functions is the ability to structure, measure, analyze, and plan. They are often inclined to want to "measure twice and cut once." Their strength can also be their weakness. For instance, people and functions with an objective knowledge orientation can be inflexible when exceptions are needed in a changing environment. Those with a strong Design orientation can be brilliant with details yet miss the bigger picture—especially when there is a change in the environment. They are sometimes slow to realize that not everything that counts can be counted and that not all that can be counted actually counts.

The Design step will be dysfunctional if it is not connected to Envision, Build, and Operate. When it *is* integrated, it can help individuals-functions-organizations focus on and achieve their goals [112] better and faster. The Design work-behavior area can also help companies establish and maintain their product-service integrity [113] by codifying customer requirements and ensuring that customer promises are kept.

The Design work-behavior area is needed to help Enterprises productively focus their resources to implement the firm's vision through clear plans and objective measures. There are several important areas that should be understood and synthesized to properly manage this step:

- The nature of the Design work-behavior area

- Using Design to improve your Enterprise productivity

- Replacing your plan with planning

- Designing your customer-centered product and service menu

- Designing better productivity into your decision architecture

- Designing better productivity into your incentive architecture

- Designing better productivity into your organizational logic

- Numbers, facts, and truth

The nature of the Design work-behavior area

Peter Drucker was the father of *Management By Objectives* [91], and much of what he emphasized was Design-oriented [3]. He recommended that Enterprises define and focus on the task, define results and quality, and demand accountability. This inclination to improve knowledge work productivity through objective knowledge techniques—the nature of the Design step—is consistent with Scientific Management [21] and the objective nature of business education throughout the 20th century.

The Design step is not a standalone component in the knowledge work productivity system. It is the bridge that converts the output of Envision into a clear set of priorities, so that the Build step can then produce an effective and efficient Enterprise structure. Design is the objective planning and measurement mechanism needed to quantify expected results, available resources, and specific deadlines.

A productive Design step requires focus. Less is more. Having too many plans and measures will make it difficult for companies to productively implement the Build and Operate steps. Remember: not everything that can be counted counts.

To illustrate this through an example, when I was head of manufacturing and logistics and then chief financial officer of Coca-Cola Beverages Ltd. in Canada, our executive team limited all Enterprise operating measures to ten unchanging reports. If a measure wasn't on one of those ten one-page reports, we didn't focus on it in management meetings. At times, local operators resisted this because it limited their flexibility when the key indicators weren't doing so well. Nonetheless, we stayed the course because this helped focus and integrate the key people—as individuals and as a group—who were in charge of running the company. When the measures were good, we celebrated together. When the measures weren't good, we jointly worked on problem solving. But, no matter what, we never changed the goalposts.

As chief financial officer I also found that less was more with investment analysts. The clearer our measures became, the more focused the company became, and the easier it was for external stakeholders to understand our value proposition. Our value model was the same for internal employees as it was for the external investment and banking communities. It focused on a few drivers. In our case they were Economic Value Added, Gross Profit Growth, SG&A Percentage, Return on Assets, and Free Cash Flow. Our value drivers were linked to the company's five strategic initiatives put in place to improve them. This worked well. The market value increased seven-fold in five years. Yes, less is more.

Staying focused on the Enterprise view is very important. This is especially true in the Design step. Managers who get consumed by too many Design-oriented details often become so focused on the parts that they lose sight of the big picture. By focusing on the pennies it's easy to lose sight of the big dollar opportunities. As I once heard a colleague say sarcastically, "They know the price of everything, but don't know the value of anything."

Skipping dollars to save pennies is especially problematic when executives don't factor in the cost of time. As a consultant, I once watched from afar as a company took a year and a half to analyze and negotiate a $1 million per week multi-year savings opportunity. If time had been properly factored in, it would have been clear that the few million that they saved through extensive price negotiations resulted in $75 million in opportunity costs. Sadly, the procurement officer viewed their detailed process a success because he did not look at the bigger picture.

A big picture view is critical for reinvention, and reinvention drives sustainable competitive advantage over time. Holistic mindsets produce very different knowledge work behaviors when compared to cutting costs every year within an outdated business model. Unfortunately, there have been many Enterprise casualties over the years when business climates changed, and managers responded by trying to reduce the cost of their firm's historically successful model.

In retailing, Woolworth did not break away from Main Street when Sears entered the malls. K-Mart took over from Sears with its city orientation, but was then unable to beat Walmart when Sam Walton's company moved in from the rural areas. Watches are another example. In the early 1800s the Swiss took over market share leadership from the United Kingdom with the first pocket watch. The United States began selling more watches by producing them with machines in the mid-1800s. The Swiss took over again in the 1900s with more stylish machine produced watches, and in the 1970s Japan took over with quartz watches.

When the business changed, new leaders emerged. Those left behind lost sight of the bigger picture and kept trying to make their tried and true business approach more efficient while their competitors were implementing a new value proposition altogether. Sticking with established business models too long is a negative byproduct of an objective knowledge orientation, causing managers to resist new approaches because they don't fit with their pre-established beliefs about how the world works [114, 115]. This often proves to be dangerous in changing business climates and underscores the importance of linking the objective nature of the Design step to the more subjective Envision step in the knowledge work productivity system.

Being clear about your business model is a consistent theme in this book. However, given the ever-changing global marketplace, there is also the need for a certain amount of ambivalence [116]. Blind acceptance of or pure resistance to new *and* established ideas is dangerous. Productive ambivalence requires that managers proceed cautiously while acknowledging, and to some degree embracing, both the positive and negative aspects of a change. Doing this can produce better answers. Had K-Mart been more ambivalent and been more open to the merits of rural stores as part of the mix they might have acted differently when Walmart emerged. Productive ambivalence is effective in complex situations when it is clear that there is no perfect answer. It can create better and more sustainable solutions by forcing individuals, functions, and organizations to embrace opposites—as long as they don't get stuck in the process.

When it comes to improving business models, there is nothing more silent than yesterday's applause. The failure of Enterprises is commonly the result of having a poor fit with the new order of things. Improving this fit needs to be continually incorporated into the Design work-behavior area through the Envision step. As a practical matter, new ideas don't need to be an all or nothing deal. There is nothing wrong with thinking big and differently, and then first testing the water with a small, isolated, and low-risk prototype.

If your business model doesn't adapt over time, your company risks getting caught in a competency trap where the world no longer values what you used to do. When this happens, watching the pennies won't make the dollars take care of themselves. It is much more likely that if you lose sight of the big picture, the details of the business will consume you—like the recreational chess player versus the Grandmaster described earlier. When the Design work-behavior area is unproductive, the business will run you and you won't be able to productively run and reinvent your business. Details are important, but as Mary Poppins told young Michael Banks, "Enough is as good as a feast."

Using Design to improve your Enterprise productivity

Productively managing and changing complex Enterprises requires a clear Design. Enterprises need to do a few things, do them well and in the right sequence, and then make them the foundation for the future [117]. From a cybernetic perspective, productive Designs keep Where you intend to go and Why in front of What you are doing and When. It then keeps How [118, 119] you are going to best do those things in front of Who is responsible for which tasks.

Enterprise Designs need to ensure that there are no gaps in the Envision, Design, Build and Operate steps. They also need to make certain that the proper sequence is in place between Envision-Design-Build-Operate. As with the other work-behavior areas, balance is needed. If Design is insufficient, Enterprises will suffer from false starts and quality problems. If there is an overabundance of Design, companies will suffer from analysis paralysis and, in the pursuit of a "perfect plan," important work will never get executed.

One example of an overabundance of Design is when companies try to track too many details in their customer relationship management systems. Since these systems can technically track just about everything, numbers-oriented companies sometimes try to force their sales people to track every single thing that they do. Unfortunately, what's possible to track in the Design step can begin to drive out what's important to do in the Operate step. Over time, this can keep sales people from selling as much as they otherwise would and make the best sales people not want to work there. To add insult to injury, firms almost always find—eventually—that they can't get consistent information when they try to make too many people track too many things. With an overemphasis on Design, they are left with information systems that have bad data and sales organizations that have bad attitudes.

Replacing your plan with planning

General Dwight D. Eisenhower viewed plans as nothing and planning as everything. Consistent with this, productive Design work-behavior areas need planning mechanisms that keep the Envision, Build, and Operate steps connected and resilient in ever-changing environments. To do this productively, large Enterprises can learn from small ones.

In small companies, when plans aren't competitive, the marketplace forces those plans—and sometimes the companies themselves—to die a natural death. In large companies, however, internal plans often aren't forced to adapt quickly enough. Bad plans, in effect, get subsidized by fixed internal budgets [120]. In unproductive Enterprises, contrary to Eisenhower's approach, the plan becomes everything and planning becomes nothing. To improve knowledge work productivity and Enterprise reinvention, it is important for planning to adapt holistically as changes occur inside and outside the company. New things will need to be started and certain old things will need to be stopped. In this regard, never put off until tomorrow what you can forget about entirely.

The Envision step needs to ensure a consistent destination [87, 88, 121] through a clear and stable vision, so that the Design step, through productive planning, can help turn that vision into a recipe that can be executed. This interdependence between Envision and Design is important so that companies can focus on the right things at the right time to productively direct scarce human, capital, and technological resources in changing competitive environments.

Productive planning needs to help companies structure their capabilities so that they can be systematized (in Build) and executed (in Operate) in a way that works well for customers and the company itself. Doing this successfully and sustainably will require that Enterprises link planning efforts to a well-designed customer-centered product and service menu.

Designing your customer-centered product and service menu

Chapter Three emphasizes that customer value and innovation are at the heart of a productive Enterprise strategy. Linked to the customer-centered strategy in Envision, an important driver in the Design work-behavior area is your product and service menu [122, 123].

Your Enterprise product and service menu needs to do for your company what a dinner menu does for a restaurant. It makes it possible to establish a formal architecture to integrate the activities of your company, customers, employees, and suppliers. If restaurants didn't explicitly and carefully design their dinner menus, their waiters, waitresses, kitchen personnel, and suppliers could not function productively. The restaurant's operations would be chaotic and patrons would become confused and dissatisfied. Imagine how difficult it would be for McDonald's to operate if there were no menu. There would be little organizational logic, from procurement to the point of sale.

In large companies, across every industry, Enterprise product and service menus often are not clear enough. Sometimes they don't exist at all. As a result, knowledge work is less productive than it can be, reinvention is not as straightforward as it should be, and scarce resources get wasted.

Enterprises need to objectively define and integrate their products and services. Each product or service needs to have a distinct reason for being, a clear target audience, and a clear message [124-128]. The product and service menu also needs to be linked to your customer's strategy to help them lower their costs and make them more successful. Finally, it's important to incorporate measurements for what your customer values and how this connects to what you and your competitors are providing and *not* providing.

Designing a productive product and service menu will force your company to objectively label itself. This can be difficult because people don't like being pigeonholed. Nonetheless, these boundaries—and the focus they ensure—are important to achieve at least one sustainable competitive advantage. Once your company labels itself through its product and service menu, you can define and execute the rest of what you do more productively. Similar to a restaurant. If your Enterprise can't label itself, you will end up getting labeled anyway—in a negative way by more focused competitors.

The value of a clear product and service menu design is most obvious with start-ups. It is just as important with large companies, but with small companies the impact can be seen more clearly and more rapidly. There is a natural temptation to try to be everything to everyone so that no options are blocked. What start-ups quickly find out is that if they want to scale their businesses, they need to label their companies very clearly, and be explicit about what their Enterprise does and doesn't do. If small companies aren't clear about their product and service menu, it is hard to be good at—or known for—anything important.

In large companies, the temptation to be all things to all people can be even harder to resist because these firms have many customers and a lot of resources. It takes longer to see the negative impact, but when there is product and service confusion, it will undermine internal productivity and external success. The inevitable outcome will be inroads by more focused competitors. Unfortunately, in the short run, this often gets masked by the revenue that established Enterprises initially receive when they expand beyond their knitting.

As part of the Design work-behavior area, the product and service menu is an important control mechanism to help Enterprises achieve constancy of purpose, continuous improvement [129], and sustainable competitive advantage. Being great at the basics is a superior idea [130], as good things will usually happen when Enterprises do less, but do it better.

Planning *What you need to do and When* through your customer-centered product and service menu is a productive way to reinvent your Enterprise and improve your company's profitable growth rate. It should be holistically linked to the knowledge work productivity system, including your Envision-based destination, Build-based structure, and Operate-based relationships [62].

Designing better productivity into your decision architecture

In addition to your well-designed product and service menu, a clear Enterprise decision architecture [131] is needed to improve knowledge work productivity on a sustainable basis. Organizational decision-making rules need to be clearly designed [132] so that companies can make and implement productive choices with respect to their goals, priorities, and organized abandonment efforts [43].

In large Enterprises, it's common to hear complaints that executives aren't good at making timely decisions and that important projects get delayed as a result. More often than not, the problem isn't a decision ability issue. Rather, there are typically systemic breakdowns up and down the organizational hierarchies and between functions. This makes productive decision making very difficult, especially when tradeoffs are required.

With Enterprise decision making, the invisible, holistic, and ever-changing nature of knowledge work is often problematic. Due to structural breakdowns, decision-making requirements frequently don't reach the appropriate decision makers in a timely way or actionable form. People on the front line assume that their bosses know more than they really do about what decisions are needed—as if some type of mindreading is taking place by the powers above. At the same time, bosses commonly assume that if and when their help is needed, they will be asked for it in clear terms. Enterprise decision making commonly struggles because both sides don't know what they don't know.

Decision-making architecture is one part of the problem. Communication style is another. People on the front line often don't think or talk in terms of decisions. They are more likely to think and talk in terms of problems. With knowledge work, bosses generally don't have the expertise of the person doing the work, nor do they have the time to acquire it. For this reason, bosses are usually not in the best position to solve problems. They *are* in an excellent position to make tradeoff decisions, however, because they have organizational power and a broader view. Even though decision making is different from problem solving, good decisions ultimately solve problems.

Productive decision making requires organizational focus, clear decision rules, and visible deadlines. It benefits from fewer moving parts and well-established escalation rules. Often, too many people are entitled to delay a decision, it's not clear enough who is entitled to make one, and there's not enough clarity around when decisions need to be made.

To be more productive, Enterprise decision architectures should ensure that decision makers are provided a short problem statement that includes two or three alternative decisions with expected positive and negative implications. These problem statements need to be sufficient, not perfect. A mechanism is also required for escalation when decision deadlines are not met, based on pre-established rules. Facilitation, using an independent expert, can also improve this process because hierarchies and functions are largely designed to protect themselves against tradeoff risks. Independent facilitation can help Enterprises navigate these naturally embedded decision barriers more productively.

There are also several other important decision guidelines to factor in. As a boss, if a decision is well within the boundaries you control, it is best not to delegate it if you know more about the subject than your employees. Once it becomes routine, it can *then* be productively delegated. At the same time, bosses will benefit from delegation if their employee has more expertise in the particular area. Delegation should not, however, be mistaken for abdication. Delegated decisions need to be a joint effort between the boss and the expert. Otherwise, the decisions won't get made or they won't be effectively implemented.

The French Emperor Napoleon Bonaparte said that nothing was as difficult or precious as making a decision. In the invisible, holistic, and ever-changing world of knowledge work, this is especially true. Decisions are steps that move Enterprises toward their future visions [31]. Your vision will determine your barriers, and your barriers will identify your required tradeoff decisions. An explicit decision-making architecture will help you make those tradeoff decisions much more productively.

Designing better productivity into your incentive architecture

Enterprise decision architectures are needed to accelerate knowledge work on a day-to-day basis. In conjunction with this, Enterprise incentive designs are required to improve knowledge work productivity over the longer term. To improve Enterprise productivity and reinvention on a sustainable basis, incentives need to be holistically linked to Enterprise goals. When too many activities are incented, the incentive system itself will lose its power. Similar to corporate strategy, incentive structures need to reward certain things at the expense of others.

For example, even though it's a common practice for companies to incent functional performance *and* Enterprise performance, the conflict and internal negotiation that this creates will negatively impact Enterprise results over time. With manual work this isn't as much of a problem because the parts are stable and distinct. With knowledge work, however, the whole is what matters most, and the parts are much more fluid.

For Enterprise incentive architectures to be productive and sustainable, benefits need to exceed the individual sacrifices required to earn them [31]. Historically, organizations have used three types of incentives [62]:

- Zero sum incentives, such as power

- Limited incentives, such as money

- Unlimited incentives, such as recognition

Incentive structures have generally been linked to 20th century Scientific Management [21] principles. Based on a command and control mindset, Enterprise incentive designs are usually strongly linked to hierarchy, and within hierarchical levels there is relatively little difference between what a high performer and a moderate performer can earn.

With knowledge work, personal contribution varies much more than with manual work. As a result, the incentive structure needs to accommodate variation to a much larger degree, and not be tied to hierarchy. With manual workers there are certainly differences in productivity levels. However, the range is relatively narrow when compared to knowledge work where the difference can be astronomical. A programming genius can be thousands of times more productive than someone who is an average programmer. Yet, they both could have similar "programmer" designations on their business card and have a similar salary range. Since what is going on in their heads is invisible to someone who is not an expert, one seems pretty much the same as the other. But from a contribution standpoint, they are vastly different.

Hierarchy-based incentive structures are relics of the Scientific Management era. For knowledge work to undergo a productivity revolution in the 21st century, incentive structures will need to increasingly be decoupled from organizational hierarchy. Having dual career ladders in technical functions is one example of moving beyond the traditional approach. Examples of total compensation being separated from the management hierarchy include movie stars who earn more than directors, advertising agency general managers who earn less than the creative directors, professional athletes who earn more than their coaches, and college coaches who earn more than their University presidents.

To improve knowledge work productivity on a sustainable basis, decoupled structures—from an incentive design perspective—will need to be increasingly built into the fabric of knowledge-based Enterprises. Since the manual work incentive architecture is well embedded, new designs will likely be resisted by many established companies. But, if Enterprises don't change, they will increasingly fail to compete with upstart entrepreneurs who are incented quite differently from traditional corporate employees.

High-achieving knowledge workers increasingly need to be incented within Enterprises as if they were entrepreneurs or commissioned sales people. Similar to entrepreneurs, they simultaneously need to be able to succeed grandly and fail completely. In many cases, incentive structures will need to be reinvented for Enterprises to be reinvented. If someone contributes 100 times more than someone else in the same department, the Enterprise incentive structure needs to be able to accommodate this. This is the norm in direct sales and much can be learned, with respect to incenting knowledge work productivity, from the direct sales incentive model [133, 134].

Making knowledge work dramatically more productive will require an incentive design where Enterprises increasingly become economic pass throughs, as described in Chapter Eight. High achievers will need to be directly incented based on their relative contributions to a few strategic drivers, and the company will not be able to retain more than its fair share of the rewards.

It will become increasingly important in the Knowledge Age for companies not to be able to grab excess profits. Similar to franchise systems, if a franchisor can arbitrarily take profits from franchisees, it will eventually take away the franchisee's incentive to generate superior results [135, 136]. Enterprises will need to establish a fair return and then redistribute surpluses directly to the individuals who generate them. Importantly, an economic pass through will also need to be a two-edged sword, and if the Enterprise doesn't earn excess profits, no incentives should be distributed either.

In the tradition of Scientific Management, companies commonly try to control knowledge workers with retention incentives. The problem with this is that placing "fur lined" handcuffs on people can have the long-term effect of keeping the least productive people in place while scaring off the best and the brightest—those who don't want to work for the rest of their lives at a single company. Retention incentives, if not designed carefully, can result in unintended negative consequences because the best knowledge workers produce a disproportionate amount of output. Drucker touched on this when he wrote that winning organizations would be those that attracted and kept top people—not from stock options and incentives, but by turning subordinates into partners [65].

There is no doubt that more productive Enterprise incentive designs are needed in the Knowledge Age for knowledge work productivity to improve in a significant and sustainable way. Incentive plans will need to increasingly and systematically reward—without limits—those activities and those people who are most responsible for helping firms achieve their visions. But not in a way that is tied to hierarchy or base salary. Most important, if the highest achieving knowledge workers aren't properly incented within your company, they will eventually be incented to work elsewhere.

Designing better productivity into your organizational logic

For companies to implement more productive decision and incentive architectures, their organizational logic—the genetic code for how work gets done—needs to also be clearly designed at the Enterprise level.

One of the most common organizational logic problems in large Enterprises is the lack of clarity around where the lines of authority are drawn between centralization and decentralization. Different centralization-decentralization designs produce different benefits and disadvantages, and there are organizational winners and losers with each of these designs. Also, there are new winners and losers each time these organizational designs change.

Decentralized organizations are well suited for autonomous and spontaneous local operations. Centralized companies are better at producing Enterprise-wide synergies and acting as a unified force across geographies and business lines. With centralized Enterprises, corporate functions often have the last word. In decentralized companies, general managers do. Regardless of where Enterprises choose to be on the centralization-decentralization continuum, clear organizational logic is required for high levels of knowledge work productivity. When the organizational logic isn't clear, it produces one of those two-headed creatures that can't function as well as its more focused counterparts.

Organizational logic should also mirror how capital is controlled. There is some face validity to controlling capital centrally even if organizations are decentralized. Doing this puts a control mechanism in place so that decentralized operations don't go too wild. Unfortunately, this inconsistency in organizational logic usually bogs companies down in practice. It often results in capital authorization processes that are over-engineered, unproductive, and ineffective.

Decentralized operations are held accountable for achieving revenue and operating income results. It is difficult for these operations to do this productively if they don't have the authority to invest the capital needed to achieve their goals. The most productive capital process is neither entirely centralized nor entirely decentralized. The architecture does, however, need to be clear. And, it needs to be logically consistent with the organizational design of the Enterprise.

The amount of time wasted on over-engineered capital processes can be significant. It is not uncommon for Enterprises to take a year between when someone identifies a capital need to when it is approved or not approved. In the meantime, a lot of nonproductive work occurs to justify why the capital is needed. Also, a lot of time is wasted as teams wait to find out if their request will or will not be approved—or to what degree. Meanwhile, more nimble competitors can have something implemented before slower Enterprises have obtained authorization to move forward. Much of this wasted effort can be redirected toward implementation, or stopped more productively, if the organizational logic is better.

Organizational logic is an important part of the Design work-behavior area. To make it more productive, capital, revenue, and operating decisions need to be integrated through a unified architecture. Productivity and the ability to reinvent the Enterprise will suffer when organizational logic is dysfunctional. On the other hand, companies can increase their speed and results when they have logical consistency, effective incentive structures, clear decision-making, explicit product and service menus, and productive planning capabilities.

Numbers, facts, and truth

Since the Design work-behavior area has an objective knowledge orientation, its people and functions commonly have an affinity for numbers.

Even though numbers are very important, it's essential to keep at the top of your mind the differences between the numbers and the business realities that generate those numbers [53]. Productivity often suffers when knowledge workers don't appreciate the implications of businesses being living things and numbers being historic snapshots.

Numbers are important, but it's critical to keep in mind that something important gets killed by the quantitative process. It is similar to the distinctions previously made between information and knowledge as well as plans and planning. Information, similar to numbers, is like the mounted deer. Knowledge, like the business, is more similar to the living one. The business and the numbers have many connections, but the differences are important as well. By the time something is analyzed, the world has usually changed to some degree. The gap between the numbers and the business and the facts and the truth widens over time.

When I was the marketing vice president for The Coca-Cola Bottling Company of New England in the mid 1980s, we introduced New Coke. The facts were clear that most people preferred the taste of New Coke. Research conclusively showed that 55% versus 45% favored the taste of the new flavor over the taste of the original formula. When the formula was changed, the truth was—despite the facts—that consumers didn't want to buy New Coke. In short order the original formula was reintroduced and marketed as Coca-Cola Classic.

In the tradition of Scientific Management and quantitatively oriented MBA programs, there is a temptation to manage by the numbers. Harold Geneen, who ran the ITT conglomerate [137] decades ago, was known for being truly brilliant at doing this. Even it turned out badly. At its worst, managing by the numbers can turn into spreadsheet management where the difference between reality and the company's what-if scenarios become cloudy. Rather than executives managing the numbers, the numbers begin to manage the executives. Spreadsheet management is great for what-ifs, but it's dangerous when companies are trying to achieve sustainable competitive advantage with customers. Numbers need to be viewed holistically through a customer lens—linked to Envision, Design, Build and Operate.

Productively managing numbers, facts, and the truth requires a holistic view and a degree of detached engagement [138-142]. A small but healthy degree of detachment—linked to Envision and Design—is needed to help managers stay centered on Where they intend to go and Why and What they need to do and When in the heat of the battle. On this point, Drucker himself recommended detachment from the tasks at hand [65]. In conjunction with this detachment, however, a healthy dose of engagement—linked to Build and Operate—is important to create a sense of urgency for those things that are most time sensitive, including How to best get projects done and Who should be responsible for which tasks.

The Design work-behavior area is the critical bridge between your Enterprise vision and its required structure. Once the Design step is connected, the Enterprise's structure needs to be productively implemented in the Build work-behavior area, using an objective work orientation. Where the Design step is the bridge between Envision and Build, the Build step is the bridge between Design and Operate. The Build step takes the output of Design and productively implements an Enterprise structure that helps people achieve great things with customers and other key stakeholders in the Operate work-behavior area. The Build work-behavior area, which focuses on systems, processes, and infrastructure, is the subject of the next chapter.

Chapter Five: Step Three of the Knowledge Work Productivity System—BUILD

In the Oliver Wendell Holmes poem, The One-Hoss Shay, he writes about a buggy that was so well designed, it needed no repairs for over 100 years. Then, the buggy collapsed in a heap in a single instant. Too many companies and industries go from apparent success to real failure—almost overnight—because there has not been enough continuous change in their Enterprise systems, processes, infrastructure, customer base, product line, and talent base. When companies do not build in enough resiliency, they risk facing the same fate as the One-Hoss Shay.

STEP THREE OF THE KNOWLEDGE WORK PRODUCTIVITY SYSTEM—BUILD

The purpose of the Build work-behavior area is to best implement the Design step. Its focus is to put an effective and efficient Enterprise structure in place to support key stakeholders in the Operate step. Build requires excellent project management capabilities to implement the company's structure productively—including systems, processes, and infrastructure.

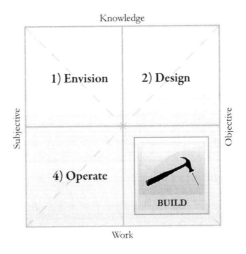

In companies, the Build work-behavior area includes functions such as manufacturing, information systems, and logistics. Build-oriented functions solve Enterprise problems through objective work. A key strength of Build-oriented people and functions is the ability to implement standard processes and step-by-step procedures. This strength can also be a weakness.

The Build orientation can also instinctively resist adapting historic systems and structures even when this is required by a rapidly changing global marketplace.

The Build work-behavior area is needed to help Enterprises scale and grow their businesses using standard systems, processes, and infrastructure. Standard structures help produce consistent experiences for customers and can reduce infrastructure costs over time. A productive Build step is especially important when companies grow—from start-ups to small companies to mid-market organizations to large firms to global Enterprises.

The Build step will be dysfunctional if it is not directly linked to the Envision, Design, and Operate work-behavior areas. If the Build step is not integrated, companies will risk having efficient internal operations that are disconnected from the market. This can result in Enterprises doing a great job on the wrong things. For example, in the 1980s Apple co-founder Steve Jobs once walked through a state-of-the-art IBM dot matrix printer facility. He commented that the factory was very impressive, but unfortunately it was making the wrong stuff. It was at a time when laser printers were about to take off.

Enterprises can do more business with lower structural costs when they have a productive Build step. This is essential to improving competitiveness, consistency, and scalability. In this context, there are several key ideas that should be understood and synthesized to properly manage the Build work-behavior area:

- Using structure to improve your Enterprise capabilities

- Integrating your Enterprise through the Build work-behavior area

- Less is more as a knowledge work philosophy

- Less is more: the Pareto principle

- Less is more: the N Formula

- Less is more: eliminating queues

- Less is more: focusing on bottlenecks

- Accelerating project management and Enterprise reinvention

- Building sustainable productivity into your Enterprise

Using structure to improve your Enterprise capabilities

Author Napoleon Hill spent a significant part of his life interviewing and analyzing people who built very large personal fortunes in the early 1900s. He found that for these magnates, knowledge only became power when it was organized and put into action [41, 88, 143]. Enterprise structure is the organizing mechanism that turns plans into actions in large companies. It does this by building a bridge from the planning and architecture developed in the Design step to the human activation that is the focus of the Operate step. Organizing a company's Enterprise structure to productively build this bridge is fundamental to improving Enterprise performance on a sustainable basis [17]. As with the other three knowledge work productivity steps, the Build work-behavior area benefits from focus, a common frame of reference, good organizational logic, and integration.

Similar to corporate strategy, productive Enterprise structure requires choices that are often mutually exclusive, simultaneously enabling and constraining how work gets done. Large companies often get tangled up because there aren't perfect choices. They want to do everything well. It's important to accept and embrace that there are things that are wrong with every choice.

What's most important is for Enterprises to move forward productively and sustainably. *Not* perfectly. Standardizing your Enterprise structure requires an emphatic choice on whether the disadvantages of standardization (i.e., lack of flexibility) are greater or less than the disadvantages of not standardizing (i.e., less synergy, consistency, and scalability). This should be linked to the centralization-decentralization decision in the Design work-behavior area.

The Build step focuses on how to best implement Enterprise structure. If the Build work-behavior area is not sufficient, Enterprises will have trouble with the quality of their systems, processes, and infrastructure. In these cases dysfunctional gaps will grow between expectations and execution. The opposite problem is when there is too much emphasis on Build. In these cases companies risk developing competency traps [144-146]. When this occurs, companies will have trouble breaking out of their historically ingrained routines when customer needs change.

In the invisible and holistic world of knowledge work and Enterprise reinvention, structure matters more than ever [147, 148]. As I highlighted in the Introduction, bad structures create bad behaviors, good structures produce good behaviors, and similar structures result in the same behaviors. This was demonstrated well by psychoanalyst and organizational psychologist Elliott Jaques. During his life he clearly established the importance of building good Enterprise structures and systematically integrating organizational roles within those structures [17, 18].

Due to the fluid nature of knowledge work and global competition, it is important to productively manage Enterprise structure because it plays such a large role in influencing the organizational behaviors in the Operate work-behavior area. Enterprise productivity depends upon structure. It requires clearly defined roles linked to logically consistent and holistic systems, processes, and infrastructure.

The importance of Enterprise structure became clear to me when I was on the due diligence team for the formation of Coca-Cola Enterprises in 1986. The company was formed by combining several large bottling entities in the United States, creating a single publicly traded Enterprise. Being on the inside during its formation, I received an excellent education on why it is so important to link Envision-Design-Build-Operate into a single Enterprise view. The bottling companies that were combined during that transaction had not been designed to work together as a single Enterprise, even though they were all in the same business. Once these independent entities became part of a single organization, the structural inconsistencies between the firms became clear. And sometimes painfully clear—especially when the company tried to determine where it was going to be on the centralization-decentralization continuum.

Structure needs to be built through an Enterprise lens to be productive—with organizational tradeoffs coordinated from the top and executed through the line management hierarchy. It is unproductive when it isn't done this way. For example, I was the first Distribution function head for Coca-Cola Enterprises in the early 1990s. At that point in time Function heads were allowed to organize functions as they saw fit. This resulted in a variety of geographic structures and hierarchical levels, which made it difficult for employees to share a common frame of reference, coordinate activities at the local level, and make tradeoff decisions.

The purpose of the Distribution function was to help reduce the overall cost of the company's supply chain. As a result, I advocated a national supply chain with fewer warehouses, less inventory, and fewer overall delivery miles required from the point of production to the point of sale [149-158]. To reduce fixed assets, working capital, and operating expenses overall, this meant that the Manufacturing function's costs would need to increase slightly to make it possible to reduce inventory buildup through more flexible production capacity. Meanwhile, down the hall, the Manufacturing vice president was being asked by our mutual boss to focus intensely on the company's production costs. He was judged on managing his costs to the nearest $1/100^{th}$ of a cent.

As we were both encouraged to go different ways, there was a philosophical conflict between the Manufacturing and Distribution functions. What the COO saw as positive tension was actually structural incompatibility. There was nothing positive that came from our conflicting directives. It's true—bad systems produce bad behaviors. When there is structural incompatibility, internal conflict will replace external focus.

During my next job I managed the entire supply chain for Coca-Cola Beverages, the Canadian version of Coca-Cola Enterprises at that time. In this case the company's CEO ensured that his direct reports were on the same page and forced tradeoff decisions when they weren't. The speed and magnitude of the supply chain changes—linked to a cohesive executive team—was rapid. Major and rapid changes happened in every function, not only the supply chain. The company rapidly reinvented itself with significant and integrated structural changes implemented in every division and function. For his reinvention work, the CEO was named the *Beverage Industry Magazine* Executive of the Year.

Integrating your Enterprise through the Build work-behavior area

It is important to have a well-integrated Enterprise structure. A productive way to achieve this integration is to link it to the knowledge work productivity system itself. Every company will be different, but the following cybernetic framework is a good starting point for company executives to begin to think holistically about functional integration.

Core ENVISION functional structure:

- **R&D/Innovation:** Capability to use research, know-how, and intellectual property to adapt

- **Marketing:** Capability to connect with buyers through your marketing mix

- **Legal and Public Affairs:** Capability to be legally and socially responsive and proactive

Core DESIGN functional structure:

- **Finance:** Capability to maximize corporate value from financial resources

- **Business Planning:** Capability to produce winning plans with specific measures

- **Accounting:** Capability to control, report, and improve financial activities

Core BUILD functional structure:

- **Supply Chain:** Capability to procure, produce, store, distribute, and service

- **Information Systems:** Capability to use information to increase output

- **Human Resources Infrastructure:** Capability to productively administer the employee lifecycle

Core OPERATE functional structure:

- **Sales:** Capability to know your customers and increase your share of business with them

- **Coaching:** Capability to recruit, develop, and connect with high-achieving people

- **Communications:** Capability to productively dialogue with key stakeholders

Given the holistic nature of knowledge work, it's useful for companies to have a shared and integrated functional view of their firm. Then, based on this view, the Enterprise's structure can be organized, integrated, and reinvented more productively. Good systems will then produce good behaviors in a customer-centered way [107]. Envision, Design, Build, and Operate should all be customer centered because your customers are why your Enterprise exists [34]. This idea too often gets ignored by too many functions because they don't share an integrated functional view of the Enterprise and its customers.

Building a productive customer interface into and across functions is important. Even though structure is largely an internal matter, it needs to be outwardly focused to be productive. It needs to make it easy for employees to help customers lower their costs and be more successful, make your company easy to do business with at every touch point, and help your people do their jobs with distinction. Excellent external relationships will ultimately benefit from excellent internal integration [159]. In the Knowledge Age, your Enterprise is your corporate brand to the outside world, and a productive Enterprise structure is its support system.

Less is more as a knowledge work philosophy

Focus is an important principle in all four steps of the knowledge work productivity system. A focused Envision work-behavior area helps make Design more productive, which makes Build more productive, and subsequently makes Operate more productive. A focused Operate step can then productively activate human relationships to achieve the company's vision with customers and other key external stakeholders.

To improve knowledge work productivity and accelerate Enterprise reinvention, a crisp focus can help companies unleash personal and organizational freedom within well-defined corridors. It is similar to how brakes make it possible for people to safely drive their cars faster. It is at the heart of what Drucker meant when he wrote about focusing and defining tasks [1, 3, 38].

In the Build work-behavior area, focus is especially important because structure is such a high cost area. It also has significant implications in the Operate work-behavior area because when the Build step is productive, this helps employees better concentrate their personal and collective efforts. It promotes a stronger bias for action [160]. For companies, this is especially important because employees are usually a higher cost area than structure and are almost always the most important value driver. To unleash the power imbedded in the *Less is More* philosophy, four management mechanisms are particularly important to understand and apply:

- The Pareto principle

- The N formula

- Eliminating queues

- Bottleneck management

Less is more: the Pareto principle

The Pareto principle, also referred to as the 80/20 rule, originally came from Italian economist Vilfredo Pareto in the mid-1800s. This principle is useful to implement productivity improvements in the Build step, because Enterprises inevitably find that a small percentage of their inputs produces a large percentage of their outputs. For example, a large percentage of business usually comes from a small percentage of customers.

This principle has broad application. A large percentage of revenue often comes from a small percentage of products and services and a large percentage of a company's transaction costs often comes from a small percentage of the firm's revenue base. Enterprises can significantly focus their structures by using the 80/20 rule. Conversely, if companies try to be everything to everyone, the 80/20 rule will inevitably work against them [161].

Reapplying the 80/20 rule over and over again upon itself is even more compelling. For example, if you keep applying the 80/20 rule to the top 20%, the top 1% ultimately creates three times more wealth than the bottom 80%. Similarly, the top 20% creates more than 100 times the wealth of the bottom 51%. Drucker emphasized this idea as well when he wrote that economic results were proportionate to revenue, while costs were proportionate to the number of transactions [34]. The 80/20 rule turns this idea into an important and practical Build-oriented tool.

Consistent with the Pareto principle, it's usually productive for Enterprises to write off underperforming products, operations, and orientations at the same time that they are moving forward with new things. Doing so can help companies establish new standards of performance [162]. It can create excitement in the marketplace with a small number of new product and service additions while simultaneously producing efficiencies in the company's operations with an even larger number of deletions.

This applies to data and other digital information as well. While I certainly respect much of the work of data miners, it can often be more productive for Enterprises to cull their information to force people to focus on the core elements of their business with customers. There are productivity benefits when firms continually update and eliminate content, because information is productive only to the extent that people can directly apply knowledge to it and make productive Enterprise changes.

Less is more: the N formula

The just-highlighted Pareto principle is an important management tool to help Enterprises focus on their products, plants, suppliers, and even customers. The N formula is another key management tool to help people better understand, communicate, and manage the complication of adding and subtracting moving parts to situations. The actual N formula is $(N^2 - N) \div 2$.

This simple formula calculates the number of possible connections between people, places, and things. For example, if you and I were involved in a project, we would equal two parts. Using the N formula, we would be able to establish that there is one connection between us (i.e., $2 \div 2 = 1$). With two people the N formula isn't very eye opening. It becomes much more enlightening as the number of moving parts increases.

For instance, if we were to go from two to three people involved in a project—a 50% increase—the complication wouldn't go up by the same 50%. It would actually go up by 200%. When teams go from two people to ten people, they don't increase their complication by only five times. The complication actually increases by forty-five times.

The N formula can help employees manage how much complication is added and subtracted when Enterprises increase or decrease the number of cooks in the kitchen, as well as the number of independent components associated with their systems, processes, and infrastructure. The N formula makes the productivity power of focus more explicit—including the value of having fewer decision makers, smaller numbers of people in project management meetings, and less complication in general.

Reducing moving parts can dramatically increase productivity. Using the N formula can help companies establish a better approach. For example, if you are implementing a $200 million Enterprise technology project, people will often instinctively believe that for such a large amount of money it had better be done perfectly, and that involving as many people as possible is a good thing. This has a lot of face validity but a very poor track record. If Enterprises change their view and focus on the fact that they are spending $200,000 per day, it becomes much clearer that a two week delay—because too many people are involved—will result in an additional $2,000,000 cost. Using the N formula, Enterprises can determine much more clearly when less is more. They will be more likely to get the right people involved faster and adopt a more practical approach. This will lead toward replacing an unproductive perfection-oriented project mindset with a more productive one of action, imperfection, forgiveness, and continuous improvement.

Less is more: eliminating queues

A queue is a line that you wait in to get service. With knowledge workers, queues impair productivity by holding up work in invisible and interdependent lines. For example, imagine a piece of work that takes two hours for someone else to complete, but is at the bottom of his or her two-week inbox. For the Enterprise, in this example, it will take two weeks and two hours to get two hours worth of output. Put four of these transactions together, and it will take the company two months to get one day of output. In the visible world of manual work, there are natural mechanisms to manage problems like this. In the invisible world of knowledge work, it isn't as easy to see them.

In manufacturing, eliminating queues is the basis for Just In Time (JIT) inventory [151-153, 163, 164] systems, and much can be learned from the JIT process when it comes to knowledge work. For example, in the supply chain area, safety stock inventory levels commonly hide the impact of supply chain dysfunctions. With JIT, by removing safety stock inventory, managers can observe and then address problems that were previously hidden—since a problem in one part of the system will shut down the entire system. In these cases the pain is felt immediately, the underlying problems are made more visible, and the issues are fixed with a greater sense of urgency. With JIT, by solving the underlying systemic problems that were previously hidden by the high safety stock levels, once the system is improved, the safety stock will no longer be needed.

Similar to JIT, with knowledge work unproductive queues are created. This occurs for a variety of reasons, including scheduling conflicts, priority differences, and skill gaps. Making the invisible nature of knowledge work more visible through mechanisms such as survey tools, open-ended interviews, cognitive mapping, and process maps can uncover queue problems so that they can be managed better. Replacing traditional meetings that require everyone to be in the same location at the same time (which creates a queue) with asynchronous communication mechanisms, such as online and telephonic conferencing tools and e-mail, can also help. The *Strategic Profiling*® knowledge work productivity instrument described in Chapter Nine is another way for individuals and teams to better manage the invisible and holistic nature of knowledge work and manage queues more productively.

The queue problem highlights the importance of interdependence with Enterprise knowledge work. For example, choices that make the individual more productive can make the Enterprise less productive, and vice versa. This flies in the face of some of the common wisdom suggesting that people schedule their personal work based on their highest personal priorities [165]. Due to queue problems, prioritizing work through an individual lens can undermine productivity at the Enterprise level. Something unimportant to an individual in a gatekeeper role can actually be very important to the company overall because of the holistic nature of knowledge work.

For example, when someone is asked to work part-time as a subject matter expert on a large Enterprise project, it's typically not the most important part of their main job. In these circumstances the individual is often inclined to put their part-time subject matter expert work at the end of their own work queue. By doing this, it has the effect of optimizing their own job while sub-optimizing the Enterprise project and therefore the Enterprise overall. As a result, someone who earns less than $100,000 per year can easily delay an Enterprise project that costs more than $200,000 per day.

One implication is that to eliminate queues, it is important to respond to people right away. Because of the interdependence of knowledge work, this increases productivity at the Enterprise level. Somewhat counter intuitively, it will also minimize your own effort at a personal level over time. If you get back to people immediately, those who depend on you won't absorb your time in other ways—including filling up your inbox, repeatedly leaving you messages, copying you and your boss on every e-mail under the sun, scheduling meetings just to get your attention, and trying to get you on a committee to ensure your involvement.

Another way to more productively eliminate queues is to use e-mail for simple communications but to talk live when the areas are more complicated. A five minute conversation can often eliminate the need for a trail of 20 e-mails over a period of weeks. Face to face is better, but a phone conversation or a conference call can often be just as effective and can be much faster when people are in different geographic locations.

Less is more: focusing on bottlenecks

Eliyahu Goldratt's Theory of Constraints [26, 166] focuses on manual work bottleneck management. An important insight in his work is that if everyone is working on their piece of the system 100% of the time, the system overall will be inefficient. For example, when everyone is working at their capacity, one part of the system will eventually be producing too much and, at the same time, another part of the system will be short resources.

Because of the role of interdependence, when one of ten implementation priorities is not moving fast enough, it will create a bottleneck and slow down the entire project. When this happens, there will simultaneously be areas that get more *and* less resources than they need at a given time. Bottlenecks are a sign that a priority is being constrained. Knowledge work can be made more productive if there is a mechanism to identify and address bottlenecks on an ongoing basis. This needs to be managed at the project or Enterprise level to be productive.

Bottlenecks are actually good if you know what they are and can focus your resources on solving them. In the ever-changing world of knowledge work, when one bottleneck is solved, another one will be created. Then, the new bottleneck will need to be solved in the same way. Identifying and managing bottlenecks is an important way to productively allocate and prioritize scarce resources in a changing environment.

To the degree that individuals, functions, and organizations productively identify and manage Enterprise bottlenecks, [19, 26], they will be able to work on those things that matter most. Enterprises will be more productive as a result.

Accelerating project management and Enterprise reinvention

Accelerated Enterprise projects are the most important form of knowledge work productivity, because reinvention requires successful Enterprise projects. Enterprise projects are to knowledge work what the assembly line is to manual work. Over two thousand years ago, the mathematician and inventor Archimedes said that with a long enough lever and a fulcrum, if he had a place to stand, he could move the Earth. The accelerated Enterprise project is the modern day lever, and the knowledge work productivity system is the fulcrum for Enterprise reinvention.

Turning sustainable competitive advantage into an ongoing corporate process, requires an accelerated Enterprise project management capability combined with hard work and a certain degree of good fortune. Consistent with J. Paul Getty's formula for success: rise early, work late, and strike oil [167].

Enterprise projects are still managed using the manual work productivity principles introduced by Henry Gantt. He was an associate of Frederick Taylor, and from his work, methods such as work breakdown structures were created. They are commonly used to logically break work into visible, specialized, and stable pieces. In the tradition of Scientific Management, conventional project management practices have defined standards through organizations such as the Project Management Institute and documents such as *A Guide to the Project Management Body of Knowledge* [168]. In conventional project management thinking, quality is an objective function of scope, quality, cost, and time. Project objectives are supposed to be S.M.A.R.T.—specific, measurable, achievable, realistic, and time bound.

Many of these project management techniques still make sense today, especially for projects that are stable, visible, and specialized. In Enterprise projects that depend upon the invisible, holistic, and ever-changing nature of knowledge work, conventional project management techniques commonly struggle. They are necessary but not sufficient. Despite the best intentions when the projects begin, the conventional project management approach often takes too long and costs too much [169].

The traditional project management approach works very well when you are building manufacturing plants or other physical structures with fixed designs. It doesn't work as well for knowledge work projects—such as Enterprise technology initiatives—because these types of projects have much more social complexity.

Accelerated Enterprise projects require a different approach. Enterprise project problems typically occur when there are gaps in Envision-Design-Build-Operate, and when there are sequence problems between the four steps. For example, when people begin working on *what* and *when* before they have decided on *where* they intend to go and *why*. They also struggle when there are unresolved disconnects with the priorities, preferences, and abilities of the individuals and functions involved.

With Enterprise projects, productive deadlines, formal communications, independent and expert facilitation, and fewer moving parts can help companies manage the natural tendencies of knowledge work to fill the time allowed and for complexity to increase beyond productive levels. Enterprise project management also improves when it is done in the spirit of General Motor's legendary Alfred Sloan, when he told young Peter Drucker in 1943 not to worry about who was right but to focus on what he thought was right [65].

Accelerated Enterprise projects—integrating Envision-Design-Build-Operate—drive Enterprise reinvention. The following table summarizes several key variables described throughout this book that increase and decrease Enterprise productivity and therefore accelerate or decelerate important projects:

Increases productivity	KEY VARIABLE	Decreases productivity
Sufficient	ABILITIES	Insufficient
Known and addressed	PREFERENCES	Unknown
Known and addressed	PRIORITIES	Unknown
Clear and stable	VISION (Envision)	Unclear and unstable
Clear and actionable	PLAN (Design)	Unclear and general
Integrated	STRUCTURE (Build)	Disintegrated
Interdependent	RELATIONSHIPS (Operate)	Compartmentalized
Smaller	TEAM SIZE	Larger
Well defined	DEADLINES	Undefined
Enterprise orientation	FUNCTIONS	Specialized orientation

To accelerate Enterprise projects, strong leadership is needed [87, 170-175], combined with a consistent focus on what needs to be done the same, what needs to be improved, what needs to change entirely, and what needs to stop. Productive Enterprise project teams also need to learn by doing [118], with a spirit of action-*imperfection*-forgiveness-continuous improvement. Unfortunately, waiting for perfection has derailed more than its fair share of Enterprise projects.

Building sustainable productivity into your Enterprise

Improving Enterprise productivity requires that individuals, functions, and organizations reduce the time that it takes to get work done and eliminate the waste [176] incurred while doing it. In the 1980s, Microsoft was a software upstart that was both working with and competing with a very dominant IBM. During that time the Wall Street Journal wrote that at Microsoft eight people rowed and one person steered, while at IBM eight people steered and one person rowed [177]. During its exponential growth phase Microsoft also differentiated the company by formally critiquing itself in order to improve [178]. The firm, on a relative basis, did a remarkable job of managing its speed, waste, and continuous improvement. A young Bill Gates wrote that success was a lousy teacher and that no product could stay on top unless it constantly got better [179].

Your Enterprise structure—the focus of the Build work-behavior area—needs to continually get better. While it is difficult for companies to change structure, it needs to be done constantly for firms to stay competitive and capitalize on changing customer opportunities. When reinventing your Enterprise structure, it is wise to follow the advice of American patriot Benjamin Franklin, who said to "Write injuries in dust and benefits in marble."

From a Build perspective, it's important to consistently invest in the future and simultaneously starve or eliminate those things that are no longer on strategy. When putting this into practice as you introduce new products, it is usually worthwhile to simultaneously discontinue or sell off those products that are underperforming. Consider keeping a $100 bill on hand and, when in doubt, look Ben in the eyes and remember the significance of dust versus marble.

For you to build sustainable productivity into *your* Enterprise, continuous structural change is a basic requirement. This is needed to build in Enterprise resiliency. Sporadic restructurings, viewed as one-time events, will not achieve the same result. For example, I once worked with a large business owner who bought all new trucks for his company to reduce maintenance expenses. Over the next decade, as the trucks grew old together, the company's maintenance expenses became worse than ever.

It was an Enterprise version of the Oliver Wendell Holmes [180] poem, *The One-Hoss Shay*, about a buggy that was so well designed, it needed no repairs for over 100 years. Then, the buggy collapsed in a heap in a single instant.

Too many companies and industries go from apparent success to real failure—almost overnight—because there has not been enough continuous change in their Enterprise systems, processes, infrastructure, customer base, product line, and talent base. When companies do not build in enough resiliency, they risk facing the same fate as the One-Hoss Shay.

Beyond the need for resilience and accelerated project management, productive Enterprise structures require the effective and efficient application of information technology. I have personally managed, and helped others to manage, many large information technology infrastructures. Unfortunately, many companies—validated by the productivity paradox—have lost their way in this important area. We can learn a lot from a two-century-old idea. More than 200 years ago the Scottish philosopher and economist Adam Smith [23] defined "technology" as something that turned inputs into outputs. We have too often lost sight of the wisdom of this definition [181]. The truth is that if information doesn't produce a valuable output, it's not technology.

When I reflect on how companies have applied information technology over the years, I think back to a division office where I worked in the early 1980s. The office had twelve executives and three administrative assistants. In total, we had fifteen phones and three typewriters. With the same basic tasks being done today, the office has now added fifteen personal computers, six printers, fifteen cell phones, fifteen PDAs, and a full suite of personal and Enterprise software. In addition, they have a technology support person to keep everything running and a customer support desk. The number of pieces of "technology" has increased by more than three times to generate roughly the same output. Many companies have too often added knowledge work tools, but failed to increase their productivity with these investments. Drucker himself warned about this in 1973 in *Management: Tasks, Responsibilities, Practices* [182] when we wrote about the dangers of technological tools becoming ends in themselves producing "information that nobody wants, nobody needs, and nobody can use."

· With the Build work-behavior area, it is important to productively implement systems, processes, and infrastructure and do a better job of turning inputs into outputs for employees, customers, and other key stakeholders. Linked to the Envision and Design steps, the Build step is an important bridge to the fourth part of the knowledge work productivity system, the Operate work-behavior area and the subject of the next chapter.

Chapter Six: Step Four of the Knowledge Work Productivity System—OPERATE

"To improve knowledge work productivity, Enterprises need leaders who set the tone, connect with people's personal lives, support people when they struggle, provide levity in difficult times, and properly motivate people to achieve the firm's vision. Motivation requires the combination of emotions and communications. As humans we all need to be treated fairly, trusted, have a chance to grow, and have a vision that is larger than ourselves."

Chapter Six

STEP FOUR OF THE KNOWLEDGE WORK PRODUCTIVITY SYSTEM—OPERATE

Envision clarifies your destination, Design converts it into a plan, and Build makes that plan possible with the appropriate Enterprise structure. The Operate step is now needed to activate the system in its entirety through people and personal relationships. This fourth work-behavior area completes the cybernetic trip around the U.S. that we began in Chapter Three. We had our brainstorming session in Seattle, crunched numbers in Boston, built infrastructure in Miami, and now need to cultivate relationships through the Operate step in Los Angeles, the last leg of our knowledge work productivity and Enterprise reinvention journey.

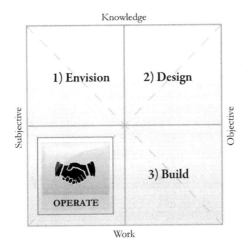

Operate—the Southwest *subjective work* step—is focused on personal relationships and human potential. It is at the heart of why people prefer or don't prefer doing business with companies. Following

Envision-Design-Build, the Operate work-behavior area closes the circuit and starts the engine. Even though it is the fourth step in the process, it is the first and most important step that customers and other key stakeholders see and experience.

The term Operate refers to the way people personally interact with and relate to one another at every human connection. It results in people being *positively* thought of as smooth operators, because they can skillfully apply the human touch, even under difficult conditions. In companies, the Operate work-behavior area includes functions such as sales, customer support, coaching, and communications. Operate-oriented people solve problems through subjective work. They are often known for being instinctive and hands on.

A key strength of Operate-oriented people is the ability to live in the moment and handle complicated personal situations. They can often energize people, and they also tend to get energy from being with people. Similar to the other work-behavior areas, their strength can also be their weakness. In large companies, too much spontaneity can take Enterprises off strategy, produce inconsistent interactions with stakeholders, and result in customer promises that can't—or shouldn't—be made or delivered.

Operate people and functions are often good at fighting fires and this is a mission-critical skill if you're in the middle of a blaze. They are also the most likely to say what people want to hear in order to maintain personal relationships. Ironically, this can make Operate people very likeable but at the same time less trusted. Gifted politicians and sales people are commonly Operate-oriented people.

When the Operate work-behavior area is weak, symptoms include poor relationships with employees, customers, and other key stakeholders. Consistent with the other work-behavior areas, the Operate step can also be overemphasized. For example, Enterprises can become unproductive when there is too much internal coddling, creating a laissez-faire climate for employees and uncompetitive deliverables for customers. In cases like these, employee morale gets disconnected from Enterprise results, and this allows competitors to make inroads over time.

This seemingly happened at the Xerox Palo Alto Research Center from the early 1970s through the mid-1980s. The company's research center during this period was truly remarkable, and the very talented group of researchers invented the computer mouse, computer windows and icons, the laser printer, and the local-area network.

Unfortunately, during this time, Xerox's U.S. copier market share dropped from 85% to 13% due to inroads from Japanese competitors [183]. While the Research Center's computer innovations were remarkable and the researchers were highly motivated, they were also off strategy. People were happily working on the wrong things, given Xerox's strategy at that time. Envision-Design-Build-Operate were not linked. While it has been argued over the years that Xerox should have changed the business it intended to be in, the fact is that it didn't. As a result, its research center efforts were unproductive for the customers that paid the bills. Researchers were highly motivated, working on things that were not connected to their company's business strategy, and key customers quickly bought elsewhere.

Lou Gerstner, when he was CEO during the turnaround of IBM, did not allow his company to follow the same path. For example, he made the IBM Almaden Research Center in San Jose, California, redirect efforts toward commercial priorities even though this rubbed many researchers the wrong way. During his time at the helm, Gerstner reinvented IBM. He took a fallen star and successfully reinvented and reinvigorated it.

A productive Operate work-behavior area is needed to help Enterprises achieve positive and sustainable results with and through people [106]. As part of this step, executives need to reflect on two important Operate-oriented questions [62]: First, how do employees feel about working here? Second, how do customers feel about buying here? Both are important for companies to be productive and achieve competitive advantage in a sustainable way.

Through the Operate step, companies can grow their businesses with customers and reinvent their Enterprises with employees more productively. As part of this process, there are several important areas to consider and synthesize to best manage the Operate work-behavior area:

- Productively integrating abilities, preferences, and priorities

- Creating value *with* customers, not only *for* them

- Engaging informal and formal organizations

- Institutionalizing coaching versus training

- Elevating the status of emotions and communications

- Activating the human spirit

Productively integrating abilities, preferences, and priorities

Better knowledge work productivity and Enterprise reinvention requires that corporate and personal priorities, preferences, and abilities be made more visible so they can be better managed. First, abilities need to be understood in the context of the work to be done. Second, understanding personal preferences is also important because when people get energy from their work, they will do it more productively. Third, priorities need to be made especially clear due to the invisible, holistic, and ever-changing nature of knowledge work.

Enterprise abilities, preferences, and priorities are ultimately managed using personal relationships and social networks [9]. Personal relationships are also the vehicle through which companies create value with customers [184], employees, and other key stakeholders. Business happens through people, and Enterprises can only be productive over time if their personal relationships are also productive [31].

Drucker wrote [3] that knowledge workers need to be treated like assets rather than costs and that attracting and keeping the best knowledge workers is mission critical. With manual work, people are also very important [21], but employees aren't the unit of production in manual work to the same degree that they are with knowledge work. For knowledge work to be made more productive, people need to be very good at what they do, know what *to* do, and get energy from what they do. Abilities, preferences, and priorities create the personal and organizational catalyst for achieving this.

Creating value with customers, not only for them

Creating value *with* customers is critical so that you *and* your customers can be more successful. As part of this, it is important for customer relationships to be interdependent and synergistic. This requires that employees understand and capitalize on your customer's strategy, measures, business model, and expectations—to increase your customer retention and revenue growth rates over time.

To productively manage the Operate work-behavior area, Enterprises need to strive for deep customer relationships. As part of this, decision makers should be lined up between the firms so that strong personal and corporate relationships can be established and nurtured to the benefit of both parties. Productive customer relationships require several ingredients:

- Understanding your customer's strategy

- Being clear on how you can help customers reach their personal goals

- Jointly agreeing on measures and working together to achieve and exceed them

- Knowing and enjoying people—from the mailroom to the boardroom

- Showing your interest in important customer activities outside of work

- Enjoying selling—because a great sale is also a great purchase

Customer relationships can be especially productive when they are modeled after strong alliance structures [185, 186]. To be successful, both sides need to benefit on a sustainable basis [127], the relationship should foster a surplus mindset [31, 127], and there should be an agreed upon exit path [185]. As part of the relationship, it is important for Enterprises to deliver a consistently good customer experience, help customers do their job better, foster community [187], formally communicate, and visibly appreciate the privilege of conducting business together [188].

Productive relationships are vital knowledge work assets [184, 189]. They require all four steps of the knowledge work productivity system— Envision-Design-Build-Operate—and need to foster community [187] at every touch point possible.

It's important to remember that customers are not loyal to companies, they are loyal to people. People are not loyal to their hospital, they are loyal to their doctor. Productive Enterprises therefore need to be filled with great people who have excellent capabilities. Creating value *with* customers—not just for them—requires Enterprises to integrate their vision, plan, structure, and people. Finally, if it's ever time to terminate the relationship, don't try to hang on past the point where value is no longer being created. With a proper and productive exit, it won't be "goodbye." It will be "until we meet again."

Engaging informal and formal organizations

To navigate productively it's important to factor in that organizations are both chains of command and networks of communication. Chains of command are visibly linked to formal organizational charts, whereas networks of communication are invisibly distributed through various formal and informal relationships.

Based on the traditions of Scientific Management [21], formal organizational structures are designed to manage the visible, specialized, and stable nature of manual work. With the invisible, holistic, and ever-changing nature of knowledge work, informal networks deserve special attention.

In business school and in business overall, there is *not* a lot of attention paid to informal organizations. Yet, it is the informal organization [31] that often matters most when it comes to getting knowledge work done productively. Sometimes you hear about informal organizations when people say, "It isn't *what* you know it's *who* you know." People with objective knowledge orientations sometimes scoff at this notion. People with subjective work orientations—the nature of the Operate work-behavior area—are more likely to appreciate its importance.

In times of stability, informal organizations often exist under the radar screen. They become much more visible in times of change. Informal organizations commonly emerge when someone is hired, fired, or promoted. Or, when there is a merger, acquisition, or restructuring. Despite the best attempts at implementing completely objective human resources policies and procedures, the truth is that pre-established familiarity, trust, and respect generally drive organizations, especially in times of change.

The informal organization comes by its nature honestly. All organizations begin as informal structures [31] and then formal veneers are added over time. For example, Bill Hewlett and Dave Packard started informally in a Palo Alto garage in the late 1930s and built a very large formal organization over time. This was also true with Steve Jobs and Steve Wozniak of Apple, Bill Gates and Paul Allen at Microsoft, and Larry Page and Sergey Brin with Google. Organizations are always informally constructed and then formally reconstructed later [31].

Informal organizations are both powerful and fragile, and they are critical to understand when it comes to knowledge work productivity and Enterprise reinvention. I experienced this as an employee when I was in my early 30s during a merger between Coca-Cola Enterprises and the

Johnston Coca-Cola bottling company, when the Johnston management team took over the combined organization. This was the first time in my career that I had been on the receiving end of a large power change. At that moment I felt like my whole world had been turned upside down. Most of the senior management relationships that I had developed since I graduated from college went away overnight. People in the formal Coca-Cola Enterprises organization quickly needed to plug into, or opt out of, the informal network of the Johnston company. Previously well established managers in the formal organization needed to informally regain familiarity, trust, and respect with the new management team.

I was on the other side of this equation when I was part of a turnaround team for Coca-Cola Beverages in Canada. The new CEO came in and largely brought in his own team, and we were a group who had known one another for more than a decade. When we arrived, we lived in temporary apartments located on Elm Street in Toronto. Later I was told that our choice of accommodations led to us being referred to as "The Nightmare on Elm Street" by some of the incumbent managers. Eventually, as familiarity and trust developed, many new and established employees came together to achieve a lot of great things.

During transitions there is often almost no relationship between what the formal organization indicates and the true Enterprise power structure, driven by informal relationships. In every company, knowing and working with a company's informal structure is critical to being productive. The difference between the formal chain of command and informal network of communication is important. In the Operate work-behavior area, individuals, functions, and organizations need to understand and capitalize on the formal *and* informal structures of their company, customers, and other key stakeholders.

Institutionalizing coaching versus training

The Operate work-behavior area concentrates on the productivity power of personal relationships and human potential. As part of this focus, coaching is an important ingredient for sustainable improvement. Across a broad base of companies, coaching and mentoring have repeatedly been shown to pay off in better performance, increased job satisfaction, and decreased turnover [190, 191]. Investing time in the Operate work-behavior area can generate large improvements [192] in productivity, especially when it's connected to Envision-Design-Build. At the same time, coaching cannot be effective in the subjective Operate step if there are not strong management controls in the objective Design work-behavior area.

Coaching is to knowledge work what training is to manual work. With knowledge work, coaching trumps training because of its invisible, holistic, and ever-changing nature. Coaching is important to winning [193, 194], and this requires that knowledge workers and their coaches co-create personal competency improvements over time.

Some people are naturally good coaches. Unfortunately, many managers are judges, cheerleaders, abdicators, or wanna-be players. Not very many are natural coaches. The job of a knowledge work coach is to use a combination of independence, senior experience, and an accelerated approach to help people identify where they are stuck and then help them make breakthroughs in those areas.

Coaches are instrumental to helping knowledge workers achieve their personal goals better and faster—linked to the Enterprise vision, plan and structure. They are an important catalyst to help people improve their personal capabilities and help Enterprises to build organizational capabilities and replace old skill sets with new ones.

A good way to manage coaching breakthroughs for knowledge workers comes from the U.S. Gordon Training International organization. Using this model, knowledge workers can be systematically coached through four phases:

1. Unconscious Incompetence

2. Conscious Incompetence

3. Conscious Competence

4. Unconscious Competence

The first step of the knowledge work coaching process begins with a state of Unconscious Incompetence. In this phase the personal coach needs to be able to see what the employee can't, using their experience and independence. People are Unconsciously Incompetent when they don't know what they don't know. For example, many managers are Unconsciously Incompetent in that they spend too much of their time working "in" their function when they need to be working more "on" their function. Working more *on* a function is important so that it can increasingly be run through other people, giving more managers the opportunity to develop their abilities for succession planning purposes.

The first breakthrough that employees need to make with their coach is to go from Unconscious Incompetence to Conscious Incompetence. At this step knowledge workers know what they don't know. It tends to be very uncomfortable, but it is an important growing pain. This phase can be related to learning to ride a bicycle. Trying to simultaneously focus on balancing, pedaling, and steering isn't easy if you haven't done it before. In the previous "working *on* the function" example, the coach will need to help the executive with skills such as time management and delegation.

The second breakthrough needed is for the coach and the employee to move from the Consciously Incompetent phase to become Consciously Competent. At this stage people can do what they need to do, but it takes conscious effort. Going back to the bicycle analogy, at this point they are riding the bike but are still a little wobbly. In the "working *on* the function" example, the coach will simply need to encourage the employee to keep on keeping on and do this from a distance.

The final stage of successful knowledge work coaching is to move from being Consciously Competent to Unconsciously Competent. This is where competence is second nature, and the employee doesn't even need to think about it—like finally riding a bicycle effortlessly. This is the phase of personal mastery. Through this step the knowledge worker and coach will have solved the most pressing bottleneck and at that point will be ready to tackle the next most pressing area of Unconscious Incompetence, consistent with the Enterprise vision and their personal goals.

Traditional performance reviews based on Scientific Management principles stop far short of coaching. With typical performance reviews bosses simply point out where someone is Unconsciously Incompetent or Consciously Incompetent. Good coaches go well beyond this to help employees make continued personal and professional breakthroughs. These coaches can be bosses. It's even better when they are independent contractors because of time pressures and the conflicts that bosses can encounter when they are both a coach and a supervisor. I once worked with a manager who told employees, "I'll joke with you, I'll laugh with you, and I'll fire you." This gets at the heart of the potential conflict when a manager also tries to be a coach.

Productive knowledge work coaches need to appreciate the value and importance of making things happen. They need to be experts on people—

to read them, motivate them, fit them together, and engage them. This requires the right aptitude and experience. As part of this, the most important coaching tools are good questions [45, 195]. They help people co-create outcomes beyond what they could achieve otherwise. In the words of Tom Landry, the legendary Dallas Cowboys coach, "A coach is someone who can tell you what you don't want to hear and make you see what you don't want to see so you can be everything you've always known you can be."

In the Operate step it is important for coaching to expand beyond a one-to-one exercise. Since business is a team sport, coaching also needs to happen in groups. Mastermind sessions are an important coaching tool to help individuals learn in group situations. The term Mastermind group was first coined by Napoleon Hill [41, 88, 143] after he interviewed people such as Andrew Carnegie, Thomas Edison, and Henry Ford to discover their secrets of success. Hill observed that Mastermind groups were a defining factor for many successful people and Enterprises because they helped those with different knowledge bases and skill sets to focus on a common goal. By doing so, they accelerated personal and team growth and produced better Enterprise results. And, this produced great prosperity.

In the consulting practice that I founded, we use Mastermind groups frequently. They help people with diverse knowledge bases discuss issues rapidly and come up with better and more actionable answers as a group than we can accomplish as individuals. Mastermind sessions are very productive from a knowledge work productivity perspective. They are almost always done via a conference call on short timeframes. On average, these Mastermind calls—often dealing with extremely complicated issues—take less than sixty minutes each. I often contrast these Mastermind calls to many three-day offsite meetings I've attended in the corporate world that achieved lesser results. Mastermind sessions have five parts, and the agenda is defined by the person calling the meeting:

1. Definition of success for the meeting

2. Agreement on who the ultimate decision maker is

3. Situation review

4. Discussion points

5. Decision to be made

For knowledge work to be productive, coaching needs to be an important part of the Operate work-behavior area because in important ways coaching is to human assets what capital is to fixed assets—it increases their value and output. Coaching was largely ignored by Scientific Management for manual work. But with knowledge work it's an important productivity tool to help people and teams break through the invisible barriers that prevent them from achieving their own vision and the vision of the Enterprise.

Elevating the status of emotions and communications

The Operate step of the knowledge work productivity system focuses on personal relationships and human potential. As a result, it depends upon emotional connection and excellent communications to function well [196]. The objective business world has often struggled with the subjects of emotions and communication. If they are considered at all, they are spoken of—in businesses and business schools—in somewhat demeaning terms such as "soft" skills.

Something that I learned as a consultant that I didn't understand very well as an executive was that the notion of command and control with knowledge workers is largely a delusion [197]. When I worked in a large company, people who reported to me would often nod their head "yes" when I asked them to do something. With regularity I would later discover that they really didn't know what I was asking for, and many times I really didn't either.

In large Enterprises these types of command and control misconceptions have the effect of making executives think that things are changing faster than they really are. After I began consulting, it became clear that co-creating solutions and building broad relationships was really the only way to achieve sustainable and productive change. It's hard, but it is required. There is probably no business management area where I have changed my view more than on this one. The truth is that with knowledge work, the command and control mindset needs to be demoted, and communications and emotions need to increase in importance.

If knowledge work isn't co-created, chances are it's not going to get implemented productively. Co-creation is different from consensus, however, because co-creation also requires a decision maker. Even though co-creating work produces slower starts, it will lead to faster and more sustainable results. Investing a little extra time *now* will save a lot of time *later* [198]. If you want something done productively and sustainably, you'll probably need to put more of your own skin in the game—in conjunction with those who are actually doing the work.

The objective nature of Scientific Management effectively bred subjectivity out of businesses during the 20th century. Nonetheless, it is very important to articulate how you're feeling so that you can better connect with how others are feeling. Emotions are important to productive knowledge work and Enterprise reinvention. They increase energy, clarity, and the productivity power of relationships [199]. In this context, key motivators include [200] the desire to win, achievement of something worthwhile, a sense of personal power, approval and acceptance, and recognition of efforts.

In the Operate work-behavior area, feelings influence actions which produces results. As part of this, it's important to remember that people ultimately love others because of how they make them feel [87, 121]. We too often forget how important the need is to be appreciated, that neglect can often be more damaging than abuse, and that if you really want to honor someone, you should ask for their help. Leaders need to lead with their heads *and* their hearts [199], and in difficult times, emotional resistance can only be overcome by a stronger emotion [26, 201]. It's important to turn negative emotions into positive ones, with special emphasis on the positive emotions of optimism, hope, faith, courage, ambition, determination, self-confidence, and self-worth [202].

In addition to elevating the status of emotions in Enterprises, communication also needs much more emphasis for companies to be more productive. This requires integrating Envision-Design-Build-Operate. Where a Design-oriented person might be overly blunt, an Operate-oriented person can instinctively be overly nice. Combining the blunt facts of Design with the emotional sensitivity of Operate is the most productive answer. In practice it is called tact. It is the equivalent in the medical world, of the nurse who has the ability to give his or her patient a shot without having it hurt too much.

Productive communications are socially negotiated. This is harder than being blunt or telling someone what they want to hear. In the communication process, it's important to connect the dots between where you've been, where you are, and where you need to go, because if something doesn't fit with the past, it will very often be discarded or misread by people. This logical and emotional transition from the past to the future is necessary for sustainability [61].

Effective communication requires leaders to ask great questions and stick to a few key points. Asking questions instead of giving orders [203] empowers people. Statements limit creativity. When you communicate, it is important to articulate what needs to stay the same, what needs to change, the steps required, and the progress being made [106]. Consistent with this, it is important to have a clear and formal communication strategy to control the dialogue and to channel formal and informal organizational energy toward achieving the vision of the Enterprise.

Focus is as important to communications as it is to each step of the knowledge work productivity system. Short-term memory is limited to about five items [204]. Three is better. If you have more than five points, people won't remember any of them. To communicate productively, it's important to be consistent, give people something that they can't get anywhere else, and make them genuinely feel wanted and loved [205].

Productive relationships are essential ingredients in effective and efficient Enterprises [62]. To activate them, the Operate step needs to help individuals achieve something as part of the company that they can't achieve on their own [31].

Enterprises need [206] leaders who set the tone, connect with people's personal lives, support employees when they struggle, provide levity in difficult times, and motivate people to achieve the firm's vision. Motivation requires the combination of emotions and communications [206]. As humans we all need to be treated fairly, trusted, have a chance to grow [207], and have a vision that is larger than ourselves [208].

Activating the human spirit

The knowledge work productivity system is an important mechanism to activate the human spirit on a sustainable basis. It requires Envision-Design-Build-Operate as a total system. All are needed to help Enterprises, functions, and individuals productively self-organize—using a unified framework and the cybernetic process.

To set the system in motion, it's necessary to energize human relationships and activate human potential through the Operate work-behavior area. This requires that companies co-create the future with their customers, recognize and capitalize upon informal as well as formal organizations, coach people effectively, and communicate with a combination of objectivity *and* emotion.

The knowledge work productivity system described in this book is critical to Enterprise reinvention. Yet, it is not sufficient in and of itself for companies to truly make the transition from being productive manual work firms to becoming productive knowledge work Enterprises. Important knowledge work company principles also need to be understood and adopted to produce the first true generation of productive knowledge work companies. These principles are the subject of the next chapter.

Chapter Seven: Productive Knowledge Work Company Principles

"Traditional Enterprises will need to reinvent themselves at a more fundamental level to compete. Knowledge workers need to rethink many ideas that have been taken for granted, are rooted in the manual work productivity era, and will eventually be unsustainable in the 21st century Knowledge Age. This chapter focuses on several of the areas that need to be reconsidered and reinvented so that Enterprises can improve faster and more sustainably."

Chapter Seven

PRODUCTIVE KNOWLEDGE
WORK COMPANY PRINCIPLES

An important benefit of the Envision-Design-Build-Operate knowledge work productivity system is its ability to help individuals, functions, and organizations manage their strategic thinking and Enterprise projects more productively. At a more systemic level, many established companies have inherited institutionalized practices that need to be reinvented for the Knowledge Age.

In the 21st century, traditional Enterprises will need to reinvent themselves at a very fundamental level to compete. Firms will need to rethink many practices currently taken for granted that are rooted in the manual work era and will eventually become unsustainable. This chapter focuses on several foundational areas to reconsider and reinvent so that your Enterprise can improve faster and more sustainably in the years to come:

- Corporate hierarchy and vertical productivity

- Functionitis and horizontal productivity

- Enterprise meetings and project productivity

- Socialized costs and free riders

- Enterprise property rights

- Asset redeployment

Corporate hierarchy and vertical productivity

Laurence Peter invented *Hierarchiology* in the late 1960s. He conducted hundreds of case studies and concluded that employees often rose to their "levels of incompetence" in organizational hierarchies. Dr. Peter found that people got promoted for doing their job well into jobs where they could no longer perform as well. This phenomenon became known as the Peter Principle [36]. During his research, Peter found that good followers often didn't become good leaders and that strong leaders were frequently not good conformers.

The Peter Principle's first commandment is that the hierarchy must be preserved. It was in this context that Dr. Peter coined the term *unproductivity*. He believed that this productivity problem in organizations contributed to Parkinson's Law, an idea that had been proposed a decade earlier. Cyril Parkinson's Law highlighted that staff was naturally inclined to accumulate and that there was a tendency for knowledge work to expand to fill the allotted time [37]. He validated the notion that too few can in fact accomplish twice as much as too many.

With knowledge workers, consistent with Parkinson's Law, one problem with building staff is that staff builds staff over time. There are many situations that I can draw upon to illustrate this, but one in particular was when a colleague described a time when she asked her assistant to make a travel arrangement. The administrative assistant called the receptionist downstairs, the receptionist called a travel agent account person, and the travel agent account person called a booking agent. The next time, my friend called the booking agent directly. This reduced her work because there were fewer misunderstandings, and in the process it eliminated 75% of the steps.

Today, at my company, Brand Velocity, our system is designed so that individuals have the option of either doing their own personal administrative work or directly allocating personal expense budgets to have someone externally assist. If we don't like to do something administratively, we either figure out a faster way to do it or the most inexpensive way to have it done through a third party. In traditional companies there is no mechanism in place to ensure that individuals pay a personal price when the Enterprise pays a corporate cost due to personal decisions. As a result, staff grows.

Hierarchies produce known problems, including the Peter Principle and Parkinson's Law. It's not productive, however, to be anti-hierarchy. Working without a clear organizational structure is the most unproductive situation of all. For example, matrix organizations, where people have multiple bosses, often translate into Enterprise versions of the Keystone Cops. Strong hierarchies are a good thing, even though we know that these hierarchies will try to preserve themselves, accumulate staff, and inadvertently produce some incompetence up the chain of command. Despite the negatives associated with hierarchies, productive Enterprise decision making and resource allocation—two keys to better knowledge work productivity—depend upon them.

Two important ways to make hierarchies more productive were formulated by Elliott Jaques [17, 18] in the 1990s. The first is to ensure that managers actively coordinate the activities of their employees so that they neither duplicate effort nor work on conflicting activities. This helps manage "Functionitis," as described in the next section. The second is to never let managers hire their direct reports. This helps to overcome the Peter Principle.

In conjunction with these two managerial principles, Enterprises can learn from Parkinson's Law. It is best if it is difficult to add staff and unpleasant to miss—or even worse, not to establish—clear deadlines. In addition, consistent with the N Formula, less is more. Fewer larger functions will self-organize much more productively than a larger number of more specialized functions.

Managing Enterprise hierarchies more holistically is one of the keys to improving knowledge work productivity and sustainable Enterprise reinvention. Organizational designs should mirror and codify the company's strategy as much as possible. And, the complexity within each organizational box should increase as it goes higher up the organizational chart, largely related to time horizons.

For example, the CEO organizational box that focuses on the next decade should be significantly more complex than a sales manager box that focuses on the next month. Dr. Jaques argued convincingly that to be productive, the complexity of the organizational boxes needs to then match the complexity of the manager's mental capacity in that box [17]. He demonstrated that for organizations to be more productive, people with greater mental complexity need to manage those with less.

Jaques' organizational work is multifaceted in its design but in principle it is simple. In applying Jaques' ideas to the knowledge work productivity system, Envision people and functions should have the longest time horizon followed, in order, by Design, Build and Operate. A common example of this getting out of alignment is when the best COOs, who were great at delivering the best short term results, struggle as CEOs when they are required to deliver the best long term visions.

Functionitis and horizontal productivity

In addition to vertical productivity within hierarchies, horizontal productivity across functions is also important to the knowledge work productivity and Enterprise reinvention equation. In large companies, functions frequently become tribes and these tribes are run by chiefs. They include chief financial officers, chief marketing officers, chief information officers, and so on. "Functionitis" is a term for when these functions become separated from the Enterprises they are supposed to support. When this occurs, horizontal productivity suffers.

Given the systemic nature of knowledge work, this is a problem because systems consist of interdependent parts, and improving one part—unless it's a constraint—will not improve Enterprise performance overall. It's easy for Functionitis to occur because functions in large companies are typically self-sufficient and well protected from invasion due to their annual budgets and organizational resources. For all of its benefits in the manual work world, functional specialization with knowledge work is often inwardly focused, segregated, limited, and even arrogant. These problems occur due to the we-them lines [40, 95, 209, 210] that people instinctively draw as they specialize. It's similar to when a puppy is trained to stay in its own yard and out of the neighbor's through a shock collar and then continues to stay put even when the shock mechanism is turned off.

Functionitis is at its worst when knowledge workers shift their allegiance from the Enterprise to their functional specialty. This occurs in dysfunctional organizations because knowledge workers—beginning with their declaration of a major in college—commonly identify more with their area of expertise than with the companies that employ them [1, 8, 95].

Functionitis is an Enterprise example of where bad systems create bad behaviors. It sometimes generates outright conflict. More often, it generates less visible cross-functional productivity breakdowns driven by incompatible priorities and preferences. A clear sign that Functionitis has taken over is when one function considers itself an internal customer for another function. There is really no such thing as an internal customer, just as there is no such thing as an internal profit center. Your focus needs to be an external customer focus.

Due to the negative impact of Functionitis, span of control principles need to be rethought through a knowledge work productivity lens. With the visible, specialized, and stable nature of manual work, a greater span of control tends to be more productive. Having more people reporting to you reduces organizational layers. With knowledge work, however, because it is invisible, holistic, and ever-changing, it is beneficial at the top to have *fewer* direct reports—so that the work between the front line and the top of the organizational structure can be better integrated.

With knowledge work, reducing moving parts at the top can systematically resolve many of the Functionitis issues in and of itself. It can also systematically improve the allocation of resources and accelerate Enterprise reinvention in rapidly changing markets. Fewer functions at the top can then make it possible to have more direct reports at the front line, and still achieve the objective of having fewer layers overall. To improve knowledge work, the top needs to be managed more holistically so that the front line can be managed more productively.

Enterprise meetings and project productivity

A third important area that needs to be rethought is the role and structure of meetings. Meetings are in many ways the playing field for the Enterprise knowledge work game. Sometimes the resulting encounters are confrontational but normally they are cordial. Attendees are typically ambassadors for their functions, sent to help if they can. At the same time, there is usually another unstated agenda, which is to ensure that nothing happens in the meeting that works against the attendees' bosses. As a result, corporate meetings systematically act to make certain that Enterprises—as a collection of functions and divisions—resist change.

Throughout my corporate career, managers often told me about their great meetings. I would instinctively respond, "What's different now because of it?" Typically I received puzzled looks. Cross-functional head nodding does not qualify as a productive meeting. Meetings need to result in tradeoff decisions and the Enterprise implementation of those decisions. As described earlier, this is why it's important that the ultimate decision maker be in every meeting that requires a decision. This needs to be the person who has authority *and* responsibility for the subject area. Also, if a meeting doesn't require a decision, it's important to question whether the meeting truly has a productive purpose.

The "meeting problem" was never more apparent to me than when I was asked to help a large team turn around a $1 billion Enterprise technology project in the late 1990s. The project was already underway and I inherited my predecessor's personal calendar. Meetings had been set up for me to systematically meet with every key person that the project was going to impact, and there were more than one hundred executives around the world in this category. I ended up dismantling the meeting schedule and two positive things happened. First, I had time to think. Second, when I requested a meeting, it was urgent *and* important, and the key people I needed to talk to were always willing to get together on short notice for this type of meeting.

Since then I have worked on many struggling Enterprise technology projects, and invariably the governance and meeting structures have been over-engineered—typically designed from the bottom up. They attempt inclusivity when the goal should be productivity. Because of Functionitis, designing Enterprise projects from the bottom up almost guarantees scope creep, time delays, and cost overruns. Overly complicated governance structures negatively impact project results. For Enterprise projects to function well, fewer moving parts works wonders.

In addition to trying to include too many people in the decision making process, the notion of alignment through frequently scheduled meetings is something that needs to be handled cautiously to avoid Functionitis. "Alignment" is a commonly used term in many large organizations. It is code for "let's get along as tribes." The problem is that for tribes to get along, no one can make a tradeoff that positively affects one tribe at the expense of another. Yet, this is exactly what is needed to reinvent Enterprises in a changing marketplace.

Socialized costs and free riders

In the Knowledge Age, it is essential to do an excellent job of systematically linking costs and benefits at a personal level. Socializing costs at the Enterprise level and personalizing benefits at the employee level create internal cost-benefit disconnects that are more problematic with knowledge work than with manual work. These disconnects give birth to *free riders*, and because knowledge work is invisible, it's often hard to know who they are.

In nations [211, 212], free riders are those who receive the benefits of citizenship without paying their fair share of taxes. Around the globe, countries that likewise receive a benefit without paying a price are also considered free riders. The European Union wrestles with this continually because an individual country can benefit from a stronger Euro while doing something locally (within a range) that would otherwise reduce the value of their local currency.

In companies, free riders lower Enterprise productivity and competitiveness by receiving direct employment benefits without paying a direct cost or making a direct contribution for these benefits. A common example of this is with executive perks or incentives that are directly linked to one's place in the hierarchy. For example, once employees reach a certain level in many companies, first class air travel becomes a personal right. Yet, if the managers were paying the difference themselves, they might be inclined to choose a seat with a lower fare. This is also true—only more so—with the use of private aircraft. I've known many executives who have been entitled to fly in company planes, but very few who continued to do so when the company wasn't picking up the tab. When costs and benefits are connected, behaviors generally become more productive. The opposite is true when they are disconnected.

Socialized costs and personalized benefits put the goals of the Enterprise and the employee at odds. This is the essence of agency theory, which focuses on divergent interests between owners and workers [213]. With knowledge work it is particularly important to link the interests of owners and workers—irrespective of hierarchy—because knowledge workers are the actual unit of production. To the degree that less productive people can benefit at the expense of more productive people, knowledge work Enterprises will put their competitiveness at risk.

To manage the free rider problem, knowledge work Enterprises need to personalize costs and benefits to a much greater degree than do manual work companies. Higher relative rewards for higher contributors, regardless of rank, is the most sustainable answer. Some might argue with this on the grounds of fairness—that people at the same level should be paid the same, or that rank should have its privileges. Yet, with knowledge work, paying for contribution is the fairest system because it is the most sustainable one. Linking perks and incentives to hierarchy pays too much to yesterday's achievers and not enough to today's.

Every company will need to strike the best balance it can between socializing costs and personalizing benefits. Fortunately, we can learn a lot from Economics. The long term danger of socializing costs too much over time was seen clearly through the much stronger economic performance of West Germany versus East Germany when the latter was part of the U.S.S.R.

During the last fifty years the U.S. automobile industry has been another unfortunate example of the long term impact of too many socialized costs, personalized benefits, and too much internal protectionism in a global marketplace. From the early days, the industry was so internally focused that it even adopted the notion of "planned obsolescence"—expecting to sell more cars by ensuring that they not last too long.

Enterprise property rights

Enterprises can benefit significantly from economist Adam Smith's thinking [23] on property rights. More than two centuries ago he worked on allocating human and capital resources to generate greater wealth and improve living standards in the manual work world. As part of this, he helped the world draw more productive lines between personal and common property. In the Knowledge Age these lines need to be redrawn.

Property rights are important to the competitiveness of nations [214] and Enterprises. From a macroeconomic perspective, property rights are protected by law and force. These rights, for example, were in doubt prior to Hong Kong's sovereignty being transferred to China in 1997. Some were surprised to see the degree to which Hong Kong ended up influencing the economic practices of Mainland China rather than the other way around.

Historically, in the agricultural age, one of the most important property rights was farmland. During that time it was proven that when farmers owned their land, the farms became more productive and everybody won. Farmers increased the output from their land since they could directly benefit from the extra work to make this happen. This surplus resulted in lower prices for consumers, and a virtuous cycle was created.

Within companies, in addition to more productive hierarchies, more integrated functions, and fewer socialized costs, productive Enterprise property rights are essential [215]. In most companies, Enterprise property rights are assigned through organizational charts, policies, budgets, formal power, and informal influence.

An important difference between manual work and knowledge work is the degree to which these property rights must adapt. With manual work, because of its visible, specialized, and stable nature, last year's property rights will often work pretty well this year. With knowledge work, in an ever-changing environment, when Enterprise property rights don't adjust rapidly, this produces waste. The past gets overfunded and the future gets underfunded. Then, new and more productive competitors emerge.

The need for adapting property rights is particularly important when companies downsize. Unfortunately, restructuring is too often done in a way that weakens companies in the short and long term. Rather than divesting what's no longer needed and investing in the future, Enterprises too often try to "tighten their belts." In the same sense that squeezing a heavy person into tighter pants doesn't make them more fit, belt tightening does not reinvent Enterprises. Enterprise property rights need to be changed for companies to be reinvented. The goal needs to be to create more value with customers, not wring out incremental profits through across-the-board cost reductions.

Entrepreneurs are generally clearer on, and more fluid with, their Enterprise property rights than established companies. They also don't tend to socialize costs and personalize benefits as much. In addition, their hierarchies and functions are generally more productive. This combination of factors makes it possible for start-ups to be competitive with larger firms, even though larger firms have more resources, broader capabilities, and more established reputations.

Asset redeployment

In addition to rethinking hierarchy, meetings, socialized costs, and organizational property rights, reinventing how fixed assets are used will be critical for sustainable competitive advantage in the Knowledge Age. As part of this, it's important to factor in from a valuation perspective [20, 216-220] that different parts of companies have significantly different financial values.

For example, conglomerates often have lower financial valuations because they lump many different businesses together. As a result, it's not unusual for their breakup value to actually be greater than the combined Enterprise. Similarly, when companies buy firms in lower-valued industries, their valuation multiples will typically go down.

Applying this notion in practice, it is important for knowledge companies to know where their value is coming from, so that human and financial resources can consistently be focused on the most productive areas. As a rule of thumb, profitable growth is the best value driver because it often expands the company's multiple (i.e., the value of a company is often calculated by its earnings multiplied by some number, which is its multiple). After profitable growth rates, a sustainable operating profit increase is the second best value driver because it gets multiplied by the company's multiple and incorporated into the company's share price. Least valuable of all are one-time benefits and the value of fixed assets, as these tend to be priced at face value.

When companies have fixed assets such as buildings, machinery, and vehicles, these are usually their least valuable holdings. Conversely, the most valuable parts of companies are often their intangibles, including brands, other intellectual property, contracts, customer relationships, and key people. Viewed through a knowledge work productivity lens, productive knowledge work is valued highest, productive manual work is valued second highest, and fixed assets and one-time benefits have the lowest value.

This leads to two important rules of thumb. First, in the tradition of manual work, it's important that your fixed assets don't cost you too much money. There is one caveat, however. If making your current assets more efficient takes top management resources away from more productive areas, you risk skipping dollars to save pennies. Second rule of thumb: in the tradition of knowledge work, it is better not to own fixed assets at all, if possible, so that they don't cost you too much time.

When it comes to redeploying Enterprise assets, it's a productive exercise to consider how you would run your company if you could have no fixed assets at all. Then, try to design your company accordingly. This idea revolutionized the hotel industry when CFO Gary Wilson helped Marriott reinvent itself in the 1980s from a hotel owner to a hotel management company. Now, it's an industry standard for hotel brands to use external partners to finance many of their physical assets.

An asset-less mindset is especially important due to the potential productivity and scalability of knowledge itself. Redeploying assets can help Enterprises focus on those parts of the business that generate the most value. It's also important to think about non-core activities in this same light. Non-core operations are commonly difficult for established companies to dislodge. I've often been puzzled by consumer goods companies that have no problem outsourcing their advertising to get the best ideas but hold on to their in-house accounting shops as if they were the crown jewels.

In the Scientific Management world, Economic Profit is a measure that applies an asset charge to a unit's profits. Thus, something that looks like it is earning a profit on the financial statements can actually be shown to be destroying economic value in practice. With knowledge work, an equivalent measure should increasingly be used to penalize activities that seem accretive on the surface until you consider the precious top management time and associated opportunity cost required to manage them.

Office assets

Architect Frank Lloyd Wright envisioned a world without large cities [32] and viewed skyscrapers as tombstones. History has so far proved him incorrect, but in a world where knowledge work replaces manual work, it will be important to rethink one of the great vestiges of Scientific Management—the office as a white collar factory.

Improving knowledge work companies in the 21st century in the same way that manual work companies improved in the 20th century [21, 31] will require a different approach. Several things need to be reconsidered relative to the historic 9-to-5 office model. First, in the global economy, it's important to factor in that competitors are plotting against you 24/7. Second, competing for the best minds is more important than ever because *great* knowledge workers produce substantially more than *good* ones. Third, with the lowest competitive barriers to entry in the history of the world, companies now need experts more than experts need a particular company. Geographically, the best knowledge workers will live wherever they want—whether your company is located there or not.

To compete in the global environment, companies can't be completely traditional—that is, working 9-to-5 at the corporate headquarters. Enterprises also will not be able to scale if they are completely virtual. In the Knowledge Age, Enterprises will need to increasingly become "Traditionally Virtual." They will need to be traditional enough to create a productive organization and virtual enough to compete anywhere in the world at any time. And, as described in the previous section, they will often need to own very few fixed assets.

Most companies have a long way to go. For example, over the past thirty-five years Enterprises have taken the most advanced information technology tools ever created and applied them to their companies without replacing their previously established infrastructures. Firms have too often added all the costs of being knowledge work companies on top of all the costs of being manual work companies. They have not reinvented themselves. Diseconomies of scale have been created, making it easier than ever for new entrants to compete with and beat established players.

To illustrate, you or I can buy a very good personal computer for $1,500 and keep it for four years. Yet, according to Gartner Research in its 2008 update of total cost of ownership of desktop and notebook computers, the average cost per year per computer in large companies is $6,000-8,000. This means that traditional companies, on average, spend $28,000 every four years for a $1,500 computer. This is driven by all of the standardized support that comes from an over-engineered Scientific Management approach—including set-up, installation, help desks, support services, and infrastructure to manage all the support.

Are the knowledge workers thrilled with the service that comes from their employers paying $28,000 to manage their $1,500 computer? The short answer is no. Some people want Macs, some want PCs, some want desktops, others want notebooks, and a few would actually rather have no computer at all. In the tradition of manual work productivity management, companies have commanded and controlled their personal technology tools in a way that doesn't work well for anyone—and at a cost that defies reason.

Many of the problems associated with applying manual work productivity principles to knowledge work have spread to the office itself. With knowledge work, however, a centrally located office is not as important as a centrally located factory for manual work. And, with the proper use of information technology and distributed expertise, it is often not needed at all.

It is still common to ask someone where their office is. Yet, we are at a time when the answer to that question has practically no meaning and where the traditional office often has more cons than pros for a large number of knowledge workers. Citrix research, in their 2007 survey, concluded that of those who do not have the option to work offsite, 62% would like to do so. Given this, where do you suppose many of the best knowledge workers are going to go? Increasingly, they aren't going to want to fight rush hour traffic every day to get to your office complex.

Applying the factory model to offices in the Knowledge Age seems natural but is unproductive. Physical proximity is not as important with most knowledge work as it is with manual work. Offices will always be with us, but how they are viewed—and to the degree that they are used—needs to clearly be reinvented through a knowledge work productivity lens.

A natural management question is, how do you control knowledge workers when they aren't tied to a common physical office? Given the invisible nature of knowledge work, if companies can't manage knowledge work outputs from a distance, they probably aren't managing them productively in their office buildings either.

With respect to offices, we are clearly stuck between the worlds of manual work and knowledge work. In the tradition of Scientific Management, similar to standardizing personal computers, it is astounding how much time, money, and energy is spent standardizing offices. Offices are also commonly tied to organizational status, which socializes costs and personalizes benefits and makes the situation even worse. With the conventional model, if someone is promoted, they need a different office to reflect this—often with an extra window, more square footage, on a different floor, and maybe even in a corner. Since benefits are personalized and costs are socialized, there is no mechanism to stop the domino effect of the never-ending office shuffle. Sadly, not one minute or penny spent on these activities benefits the company's customers.

On the human side of the equation, while offices do help to give people a stronger corporate identity, it's worth considering the dark side of how work-life balance is negatively impacted by applying the factory model to offices. What if you could give back all the time spent in the car driving to and from the office? What if knowledge workers didn't need to relocate their families so much? To what degree do flexible hours have the potential to make work-life balance better and help companies be more competitive in a 24/7 world?

There is no question that the human touch is important with knowledge work, and it must be designed into the Traditionally Virtual model. The human touch will need to be increasingly decoupled from geographic structures and then be reconnected to the teams themselves so that knowledge workers, their functions, and organizations can be more effective and motivated. Is this unrealistic? Far from it. The next generation of workers is *already* more digitally connected than geographically connected to their chosen communities, using Facebook, Skype, Twitter, and many other human networking applications.

There will always be those who require an office, and there is often no good substitute for face-to-face interaction. But, on a relative basis, just as the number of farms reduced as farming became more productive, the number of offices required to support knowledge workers will also need to decline over time. In the spirit of the fixed-asset-less company, thinking about the office-less company is also a worthwhile exercise. By reflecting on this, you may find that you are able to reduce fixed assets via Web-based technologies and a "Traditionally Virtual" architecture that eliminates the nonproductive human costs of long commutes, frequent relocations, and inflexible work hours.

Creating knowledge work productivity companies

Improving knowledge work productivity is the most important management challenge before us [1, 3, 4, 38]. To move forward successfully, companies will need to factor in that, unlike manual workers on an assembly line, knowledge workers are more often free agents [221]. This fact changes the game when it comes to creating productive knowledge work companies.

Firms in the Knowledge Age will need to capitalize on the independent nature of knowledge workers [8] with an Enterprise architecture that makes workers and employers more productive on a sustainable basis. This will require that Enterprise managers rethink their hierarchy, meetings, socialized costs, Enterprise property rights, and use of fixed assets.

Drucker acknowledged that it would be difficult to build productive knowledge work companies [3]. On one hand there is a need to start small, but there is also a need to manage the holistic nature of knowledge work at the Enterprise level. Certainly, better knowledge work productivity is needed in large companies. But, large companies have proved to be a difficult place to start and an even more difficult place to sustain progress [6].

In conjunction with the work on this book, a working model for a more productive knowledge work company was developed and prototyped from a clean sheet of paper with real customers and employees. Through the Brand Velocity prototype we were able to integrate theory and practice to ensure that the ideas were more than some hypotheses in a white paper and could also be more than a one-off experiment. Our team made the choice to make mistakes in a competitive environment rather than strive for perfection on a white board or in an academic article. In the next chapter you will see how this was done and how you can apply what we've learned to your company.

**Chapter Eight: Prototyping a Knowledge
Work Productivity Based Company**

*"There have been many discoveries while prototyping Brand Velocity, Inc.
using knowledge work productivity principles. An important one has been
the realization that the issues that make it difficult for large Enterprises to
grow are the same ones that make it so easy for small companies to fail. It
has also been clear that there are important similarities between invention
with start-ups and reinvention with established companies."*

Chapter Eight

PROTOTYPING A KNOWLEDGE WORK PRODUCTIVITY BASED COMPANY

While first reading Drucker's *Post-Capitalist Society*, his thoughts on knowledge work productivity and its connection to Enterprise reinvention struck a chord with me. I had often experienced high personal frustration when things took longer than they needed to and satisfaction when more rapid progress was made. On April 30, 2001, which was my forty-third birthday, I began to focus my attention on this full time. I have joked that this was the day that I officially declared my mid-life crisis. After more than a year's notice, and more than twenty years working in a large-company environment, I drove out of the corporate headquarters of The Coca-Cola Company and began to concentrate fully on what Drucker considered to be the next frontier of management.

Since then, I have worked to create and integrate four things. First, to develop, in conjunction with doctoral work at The George Washington University and our firm's consulting with clients, a practical yet research-based knowledge work productivity framework and process. The result is the system described in this book. Second, to develop an online survey-based instrument to help people more easily apply the system to their lives and to accelerate their Enterprise projects. This instrument is described in Chapter Nine. Third, to prototype an actual company based on knowledge work productivity principles, to test and refine a holistic set of Knowledge Age ideas with real employees, customers, and competitors. This Chapter describes the company's work on this prototype. Finally, I wanted to get all of these things completed and incorporated into a book before

Peter Drucker's hundredth birthday in his honor. This resulted in *Reinvent Your Enterprise*, the first book in a series under the trademark, *The Earning Organization.*

To build a company based on knowledge work productivity principles, I began with Drucker's notion that knowledge workers owned their means of production. Unlike working on a manufacturing line in the manual work world, knowledge is in people's heads—portable, infinitely scalable, but with a rapidly declining shelf life. Drucker emphasized that to protect and enhance these assets, companies need to retain and attract the highest producing knowledge workers and determine what is needed to increase their productivity. He emphasized *what* needed to be done in knowledge work companies but left the *how* of it to his readers [95].

As noted previously, Drucker believed that knowledge work productivity efforts needed to start small. The dilemma has been that they also need be holistic. These opposing requirements have made it difficult for firms to create knowledge work productivity based companies. Starting small yet being holistic in established companies are opposing requirements.

Despite this challenge Drucker was clear that, similar to the global market we compete in, knowledge Enterprises need to be borderless, upwardly mobile, and provide the potential for failure as well as success [5]. This can't be tested in a book, on a white board, or within a discrete consulting engagement. Brand Velocity, Inc. was designed to holistically prototype, in a competitive marketplace, the knowledge work productivity principles that Drucker suggested and that this book describes.

On one hand, a start-up was needed so that knowledge work productivity and Enterprise reinvention could be approached holistically. On the other hand, it needed to be done with people who were used to running and working in large organizations so that we could factor in the need for scalability. Among others, these executives include the previous CEO of Ernst & Young Consulting global accounts, a previous group president responsible for running one-third of The Coca-Cola Company, a previous CIO of Kimberly-Clark, and a previous chief technology officer of The Coca-Cola Company.

This chapter highlights some of what we've learned so that you can more rapidly incorporate key knowledge work productivity principles into your thinking and begin to reinvent *your* Enterprise—better and faster. As I put my global company hat on, I believe that most everything we've tested can be scaled with limited modifications. With every action we've taken, a large company view was incorporated into the design so that it can help individuals, functions, and organizations reinvent their Enterprises—large and small.

The Brand Velocity team, over a five-year period, worked every day to prototype key knowledge work productivity principles. Even though we are a small firm, we have by now invested more money than the average academic institution could spend on the subject and have dedicated more time—at a more holistic level and over a longer period—than most large firms could invest. Funded by more than $15 million of engagements, some interesting results so far are that the firm does not own any fixed assets, does not require operating capital to grow, and has a cost structure 20% lower than the consulting industry it competes in. Most importantly, our clients consistently rate the firm highly when compared to many of the best-known consulting firms in the world.

Prototyping Brand Velocity from a clean sheet of paper has required a significant amount of work. Start-up companies are a challenging proposition any way you look at it. New companies have 80% failure rates within five years and then 80% of those companies end up failing in the next five [222, 223]. Creating a company based on knowledge work productivity principles has added another degree of difficulty because—in addition to competing as a start-up—we have chosen to think through all of our work practices through a knowledge work productivity lens. But, this has been rewarding and important. With no external financing, Brand Velocity has successfully operated without a financial safety net. Yet, being dependent on client revenues to function has been critically important. It has always been clear who our customers are, what their needs are, how precious they are, and that our knowledge work productivity based capabilities ultimately need to benefit them.

Most companies begin with an idea. Ours was the belief that in the Knowledge Age the global marketplace will be in a constant state of flux. In this environment your Enterprise—as a system—is truly your corporate brand and its velocity is driven by the success of your Enterprise projects. That's why the name Brand Velocity is not marketing oriented as it would be in the Scientific Management era. It is a project acceleration company focused on Enterprise reinvention—initially concentrating on large Enterprise projects with significant information technology components.

There have been many discoveries while prototyping Brand Velocity, Inc. An important one has been the realization that the issues that make it difficult for large Enterprises to grow are the same ones that make it so easy for small companies to fail. Namely, the need to improve focus, allocate resources better, and successfully manage voids and sequence problems in the knowledge work productivity management system. It is also clear that there are important similarities between invention with start-ups [224–226] and reinvention with established companies. The success and failure of both are strongly linked to how well the Envision-Design-Build-Operate system is integrated and executed.

As I emphasized in Chapter Five, there are disadvantages with every structural choice. But, if you try to be all things to all people, you will get the worst possible result. Given a clear vision, if you try to undo your "strategic disadvantages," you risk creating an ineffective two-headed creature. For example, a company can't reap the benefits of being asset-less if it makes a decision to introduce assets to address the imperfections of an asset-less system. If it does, the company will move from an imperfect asset-less system that has a competitive advantage to an imperfect asset-filled system that has no competitive advantage.

Connecting the dots from the previous chapter, whether your Enterprise is large or small, managing your hierarchy, meetings, socialized costs, Enterprise property rights, and fixed assets should be a top priority. This is at the heart of sustainable knowledge work productivity improvement and Enterprise reinvention. Consistent with this thinking, the following seven reconstructions learned from the Brand Velocity prototype are particularly important—linked to the principles described in Chapter Seven.

Reconstruction One: Work to increasingly help your customers be more productive

"If you want something, give it [138]." One of the best ways to improve your own knowledge work productivity is to focus on helping your customers improve theirs. As part of this reconstruction it really helps to know what it is like to sit in your customer's chair. Our company focused on accelerated Enterprise projects because most of us had been large consulting firm clients, and we were able to view the consulting business through the client's lens.

To help your customers improve their productivity, it's useful to follow Peter Drucker's advice and concentrate on helping them reduce their costs and be more successful. To achieve this, five activities are particularly important:

- Concentrate your intellectual property and your product-service menu on your customer's goals.

- Make your sales and relationship management process more productive for your customers (this will also make it more productive for you).

- Link your delivery capability to your product-service menu so that there is a clear connection between what your customers are buying and what you are delivering.

- Integrate your employees with your client's employees to become increasingly interdependent and productive.

- Be a pleasure to do business with from a business systems perspective (if your systems aren't transparent, customers will focus on your weaknesses instead of your strengths).

Your customer touch points should be like the design of a good print advertisement [227] in the sense that if the reader notices the layout, it is a bad layout. Similarly, your company's systems need to—without distraction—focus your customers and your people on your client's most pressing needs and the products and services that can help them.

To achieve this it's important to implement your Envision-Design-Build-Operate system through a customer lens to make them *and you* continuously more productive and successful. Individuals, functions, and the organization overall need to work together to help customers while also achieving your Enterprise vision—by articulating, integrating, implementing, and accelerating the four-step knowledge work productivity process:

- Envision—Where you intend to go and Why

- Design—What you need to do and When

- Build—How to best do those things

- Operate—Who is responsible for which tasks

Reconstruction Two: Work to increasingly turn your Enterprise into an economic pass through

For knowledge work to be made more productive on a sustainable basis, many Enterprises will increasingly need to be reconstructed into economic pass through companies. Unlike manual work, where the factory is the source of the output, with knowledge work, individuals are the source of production. To systematically improve productivity, knowledge workers will increasingly need to be compensated based on their personal contributions, without the company taking more than its fair share through either profits or overhead. At the same time, knowledge workers will need to directly feel the pain when the goals of the Enterprise aren't achieved.

To prototype this, Brand Velocity was created as an economic pass through. As such, consistent with the last chapter, there are no caps to compensation and there are very few socialized costs linked to personalized benefits. To create this, the first step was to build a low cost structure and a more productive asset design. The second step was to retain only the amount of this cost advantage as a firm and pass through all other profits.

At Brand Velocity, there is a 20% structural cost advantage, so operating income is capped at this amount. All surplus profits are redistributed to employees based on their contributions tracked by "points" within the firm related to the company's top three business drivers: selling great work, delivering great work, and recruiting and developing a diverse group of great people.

Our use of points to redistribute surplus profits is linked to the company's Enterprise vision and the three drivers just mentioned. There are many important activities that people do and need to do. However, the key behaviors that drive the redistribution of the company's surpluses, and that we can't live without, are selling, delivering, and recruiting/developing. Other activities are important, but they don't earn points.

The result is that high contributors—regardless of rank—can earn more at Brand Velocity than they can if they start their own company or work for another firm. Employees don't need to be a consulting firm "partner" to be compensated like one. At the same time, the most senior people aren't guaranteed the highest total earnings. Compensation is contribution based and the corporation is effectively a vehicle to pass through profits to those who generated them for the firm.

To reduce the Enterprise cost structure and increase potential surpluses, Brand Velocity was designed and built using a "Traditionally Virtual" structure so that it doesn't require fixed assets. The company is also designed in a way that doesn't socialize costs and personalize benefits—including expenses related to infrastructure, insurance, 401K investment choices, individual perks, and personal business expenses. Employee base compensation and business expenses are structured in a way where, as described later, every personal choice has some form of a personal cost or benefit. This produces an ongoing operating mechanism to link the costs that the Enterprise incurs and the true value that the individual places on practically every personally-driven business expense.

In the spirit of the Jim Collins and Jerry Porras book *Built to Last* [228], continuous adaptation—being a time teller not a clock builder—is a natural byproduct of the Traditionally Virtual design. Bucking the start-up failure statistics, Brand Velocity would have gone out of business at least once had the company not had an economic pass through structure. With this structure employees adapt to conditions much faster than more traditional companies because there are direct personal rewards and penalties for success and failure. This encourages people to perpetually improve knowledge work productivity within the firm as well as between the company, our customers, and other key stakeholders.

A healthy and productive culture is critical when building an economic pass through structure. We've discovered that as an economic pass through, the company needs to be even more process oriented than traditional firms. Developing and reinforcing organizational culture through standard activities and operating procedures is very important. It is needed to help establish each employee's identity with the firm and increase consistency and productivity with clients and throughout the Enterprise. The Brand Velocity culture emphasizes being smart, hardworking, ambitious, and nice. The most unusual value according to people we interact with is our emphasis on being nice. However, with knowledge work, if people aren't nice, friendly, collegial—whatever you want to call it—their relationships, and therefore their work, won't be as productive as it would otherwise be.

Reconstruction Three: Work to increasingly decouple status and rank from total compensation

Enabling people to perpetually benefit—through rank—from past personal achievements is the hallmark of the Peter Principle, Parkinson's Law, the traditional hierarchy, and unproductive knowledge work. Linking rank, status, perks, and total compensation creates a "King of the Hill" problem. It is an Enterprise version of the children's game where a boy or girl works to get to the top of a hill and then tries to keep others from displacing him or her. The King of the Hill problem is a knowledge work productivity barrier because when rank is linked to compensation and benefits, it gets disconnected from personal contribution.

In this regard, while it's common and often even done in the name of knowledge retention, companies should be cautious when it comes to us-ing fur-lined handcuffs, such as deferred/restricted compensation. There is a systemic productivity danger for companies when their executives earn important positions in the hierarchy and are then incented to not mess up until their retirement. This rewards stability in times of change. It can also turn seasoned executives into corporate zombies, frustrate up-and-comers, and scare the more entrepreneurial employees who fear being trapped by compensation that requires a very long personal commitment.

With knowledge work, productivity is linked more directly to indi-vidual and team contributors than to those who command and control the organization. This is not to say that the CEO decision isn't one of the most important ones that boards make. However, as a rule of thumb in the Knowledge Age, if you have an Enterprise where employees aren't able to earn more than their bosses, your company probably won't be as produc-tive as it could be.

To prototype this decoupling of rank from compensation, Brand Velocity was designed so that it doesn't systematically link benefits to rank. There are hierarchical levels, but they are structured in a way that—at the most—impacts base compensation within a fairly narrow band. It offers no other advantages. Rank doesn't determine incentive potential, personal benefits, perks, 401K matches, or the ability to earn equity. As senior people contribute to the company's three key drivers, they are remunerated from surplus profits consistent with their contributions, not their title.

If a more junior employee leads the sale of an engagement, they will earn the same as a more senior employee. Decoupling rank from compensation and benefits helps the company continually improve its knowledge work productivity. It also directly rewards those who are generating the firm's profits. This is important in rapidly changing competitive environments, and since high achievers contribute disproportionately to an Enterprise's value and are not the same people from one year to another. Interestingly, so far we have found that senior people often do contribute more and earn more, but there are significant differences between individuals and from one year to another.

Reconstruction Four: Work to increasingly move from merit to contribution-based rewards

Traditional merit increases are a byproduct of the Scientific Management age and are largely a socialized cost. Reconstructing this practice is probably a bridge too far for many established companies. Nonetheless, as Enterprises have more socialized costs and personalized benefits, they will find it more difficult to compete with new entrants over time.

At the Enterprise level, merit increases systematically shift expenses toward higher-paid people, are largely correlated to rank, and tend to equalize the compensation differences between more productive and less productive people within a given hierarchical level. In the manual work world, merit increases are not as much of a socialized cost because the productivity differences between manual workers are not as dramatic and rank is more closely related to skill differences. With knowledge work, where people are the unit of production and there are large and constantly changing contribution differences, the misallocation of resources is more significant.

Merit increases tied to performance ratings are better, but they too are largely anti-productive in the knowledge work world. For example, Enterprises that offer a standard merit increase of 2–5%, when knowledge work contributions can vary more than 1,000%, misallocate resources in the short and long term by systematically overcompensating underproductive employees and under-incenting more productive ones. This is fine if everyone is happy. It's not if your most productive employees believe that they can do better elsewhere.

Contribution-based compensation is much better suited to knowledge work companies than merit increases. With knowledge workers, similar to direct sales forces, there will often be large contribution differences between people. For example, Brand Velocity contribution payout differences are often more than 10 to 1, with everyone in the company playing by the same rules.

In the future, contribution-based compensation also promises to help manage major demographically related challenges [5]. The younger population is shrinking, the older population is growing, and experienced workers have a lot to offer when it comes to knowledge work. At the same time, many people with senior experience don't want to work full time but continue to have economic needs. A win-win-win for knowledge work productivity companies, older knowledge workers, and younger knowledge workers who will ultimately be responsible for supporting the country's social programs, is to have a system that is not designed to pay workers merit increases, but pays them for contribution. Contribution-based compensation structures open up many flexible options that are productivity friendly for companies and employees alike.

Reconstruction Five: *Work to increasingly redesign your corporate and personal infrastructure*

The notion of corporate and personal infrastructure is connected to Adam Smith's thinking on property rights [23] in Chapter Seven. In the manual work world, the factory and assembly line are clearly corporate infrastructure. The property rights are clear and stable. In the knowledge work world, personal and corporate infrastructure have increasingly converged and the lines need to be drawn differently and more productively.

For example, we live at a time where it's clear that personal computers are called personal for a reason. By trying to standardize them, large corporations have stayed in their comfort zone from a command and control perspective but have paid a high price when it comes to productively allocating their resources.

With computers, until the 1980s life was pretty simple and just about everything related to data could be controlled and self-contained. It all pretty much stayed in the mainframe. Today, data transmission and storage is nearly ubiquitous [104, 229-232]. In a world filled with memory sticks, notebook computers, smart phones, wireless networks, presentation and document files, copy machines, e-mail, scanners, fax machines, blogs, Web sites, and intercompany collaboration efforts, data security *policy* needs to play a greater role [57, 58, 233-237]. By applying Scientific Management principles to knowledge work, we are too often applying $2 solutions to $1 problems.

Security standards clearly need to be designed-in from an Enterprise and customer risk perspective, but the process often gets over-engineered without significantly better security. Companies often end up being an Enterprise version of men and women who won't give their credit card number to Amazon.com but don't think twice about handing their cards over to unknown waiters in restaurants. With technology security, productive risk management needs to strike the proper balance between costs and benefits and between technical controls and policy controls.

In the Knowledge Age, where individuals are the unit of production and information technology is ubiquitous, the distinction between corporate infrastructure and personal infrastructure needs to be reconstructed. Knowledge workers need to simultaneously be given more choice with respect to their personal tools and less choice when it comes to the Enterprise systems of the companies themselves. Both have become confused and unproductive over the past twenty-five years.

Standardized personal tools and offices were required prior to the mid-1990s when networks, Web browsers, and Web applications were either non-existent or very immature. Today, standardizing personal tools often doesn't add sufficient value to cover the costs of standardizing them. The property rights problem between corporate and personal infrastructure is a large part of why the promise of technology has so often been broken and why the productivity paradox haunts us today. Companies have added knowledge work infrastructure costs on top of manual work infrastructure costs, rather than using the former to replace the latter.

On the corporate infrastructure side, Enterprises are often not clear enough on who has the right to determine what the Enterprise systems look like. This is exacerbated by bottom-up governance designs. As a result, companies create additive technology layers, duplicated systems, and incompatible data standards over time. If the chief marketing officer and a division president want different systems, Enterprises—and the poor project managers stuck in the middle—too often adopt both or some compromise that is worse than either option. To make matters even more maddening, the originating executives are rarely around as long as the systems need to be maintained. Sometimes they have even moved on before their pet system has even gone live.

Because we have applied Scientific Management principles to information technology, employees commonly view corporate infrastructure as *their* systems. They also view personal tools as the company's. In both cases this is unproductive. The command and control management of personal and corporate assets needs to be reconstructed, and a more productive distinction between corporate and personal infrastructure is required to do this.

Redesigning the management of corporate and personal infrastructure has been prototyped at Brand Velocity for several years. With personal infrastructure, as long as people can do their job, there is complete flexibility with respect to their personal choice of tools. The company advances a set amount of money to employees so that they can pay for business tools and other personally determined business expenses as they see fit. If John likes a Dell PC and a BlackBerry and Mary loves her Mac and Palm, the company doesn't dictate one over the other. Employees need to be able to effectively collaborate via the Web, ensure that data is secure, and be personally productive, but these are the only requirements.

Compared to a traditional infrastructure design, this approach to personal infrastructure makes the company much more productive with items such as phones, office space, computers, and printers while allowing a high degree of personal freedom. On the other hand, the company very tightly controls its corporate infrastructure, including its intranet, project management system, customer relationship management system, voicemail, e-mail, conferencing capabilities, document retention, and mail handling. If an employee wants to add complexity to corporate infrastructure, he or she has the right to be heard but not the right to make the decision to change it.

Personal and corporate property rights need to be reconstructed in the Knowledge Age, and everyone involved will benefit as a result. There is no doubt that by combining a better design and better management, many Enterprises will be able to significantly improve the productivity of their companies and their infrastructures.

Reconstruction Six: Work to increasingly reduce Enterprise transactions and moving parts

The Pareto principle and N formula described in Chapter Five emphasize the productivity problems created when the number of transactions increases. For example, it costs the same to process a $1 check as it does to handle one for $100,000 [34]. From a productivity perspective, fewer transactions translate into less distraction. Less distraction then helps increase focus to achieve sustainable competitive advantages over time.

Designing in fewer transactions was formally prototyped at Brand Velocity from the ground up. For example, in the case of employee business expenses, the company advances employees money at the beginning of every quarter. This business expense advance is used by employees to pay for personal IRS-approved business expenses and administrative support. At the end of every quarter employees settle up via a company expense report. Employees don't get their next advance until they have completed their prior expense report. At the end of the year, if employees have money left over in their expense fund, they write a check to the company, and the money is then paid back to them via payroll as income after taxes.

This approach produces the following benefits. First, it reduces the number of internal expense report transactions per person to four per year—a 90% reduction. Also, since employees get back everything that they don't spend on business expenses as income, they treat expense dollars as if they were their own—because ultimately they *are*. This directly connects the personal costs and personal benefits associated with the company's business expenses so that costs are not socialized with benefits personalized. This is much more productive for the company than the standard business expense approach. It substantially reduces the number of moving parts and aligns the interests of the Enterprise with its employees.

The way that personal infrastructure and corporate infrastructure is handled, as highlighted earlier, also significantly reduces the number of moving parts associated with phones, computers, printers, software, office supplies, and the like. From a structural perspective, as is emphasized in Chapter Five with respect to the Build work-behavior area, less is more.

Reconstruction Seven: Work to increasingly replace judging with coaching

Knowledge work does not happen in a vacuum. It is created by and through people. This requires personal growth and productive collaboration to a greater degree than manual work. As a result, it's important to design in personal reflection, coaching, and teamwork.

As emphasized in Chapter Six, knowledge work productivity requires more coaching and less judging than manual work. As a byproduct of Scientific Management, annual reviews are often done based on a normal curve, with forced winners and losers. These exercises are called performance reviews, and are tailored to the visible, specialized, and stable nature of manual work. There is probably nothing inherently wrong with the term, but my instinctive reaction when it comes to knowledge workers is that "dogs perform and people contribute." This is especially true with the highest achieving knowledge workers. For instance, I have a hard time envisioning how effective a performance review would have been between Albert Einstein and his boss.

Knowledge workers need to productively contribute to ever-changing environments in ways that their bosses often can't even imagine. As a result, people need personal reflection and coaching more than annual judgments. This was designed into Brand Velocity through a twice per year automated process for people to reflect on what they and the company need to do the same and need to do differently. This is combined with coaching for the employee, the boss, and ultimately the company overall.

There is not enough personal reflection and coaching in the traditional performance appraisal process. Personal coaching and personal reflection are what matter most as people continuously move through the four stages of their knowledge work coaching breakthroughs:

- Unconscious Incompetence

- Conscious Incompetence

- Conscious Competence

- Unconscious Competence

Teamwork also needs to be systematically designed into productive knowledge work organizations. This was prototyped at Brand Velocity using the points system for selling, delivering and recruiting/developing described earlier. From a teamwork perspective, when points are earned, the sales, delivery, and recruiting/development leads are required to redistribute forty-five out of every hundred points generated to the people in the company who helped them the most. This encourages two things to happen. First, it encourages "lone rangers" to work with others since they will be required to award points to someone no matter how little help they receive. Second, it encourages others to want to help since they stand to be directly rewarded points for their efforts.

This principle is carried through at the end of every year with the company's Founder's Award for the person who best balances selling, delivery, and recruitment/development. In these cases the employee is given $10,000 after taxes, of which $5,500 is theirs to keep, and $4,500 is theirs to distribute to those who have helped them the most.

Learning, earning, and Enterprise reinvention

To be more productive, it is important for Enterprises to clarify and integrate their visions, plans, structures, and relationships. First, it's important to focus on customers and employees. If this can be done successfully, shareholders are more likely to prosper as well. With knowledge work, since individuals are the unit of production, focusing on the shareholder first is like focusing on the pulse rate rather than on the heart that produces it. It's important to build a company that you would like to be part of and do business with. In a sentence, it's important to encourage great people to join, to stay, and to do the best work of their lives.

Knowledge work requires a "learning" organization but knowledge work productivity requires an "earning" organization. A learning organization focuses on improving inputs whereas an earning organization must concentrate on turning inputs into outputs. Learning, unlearning and relearning [9] is only one part of the equation. Walmart Founder Sam Walton, for example, continually learned from customers, competitors, and suppliers [84]. More importantly, he converted his learning into earning—i.e., into outputs. This is what generated his wealth. If learning alone drove knowledge work productivity, universities would be the most productive institutions on earth. The fact is, their costs consistently outpace inflation, which is the litmus test for unproductive Enterprises.

Your organization's ability to rapidly convert knowledge into action will be its most sustainable competitive weapon in the Knowledge Age. To be successful, it is important not to study good ideas until they become bad ones. Knowledge has a short shelf life and acceleration is more important than it has ever been.

To reinvent *your* Enterprise, a better structure is needed to produce better results. Importantly, when you change your structure, something will die. As part of this process, if you don't care about something, abandon it. Don't do less of it, don't do it at all. On the other hand, if your Enterprise *does* significantly care about something, it's important to accelerate it using the knowledge work productivity system:

- Envision—Where you intend to go and Why

- Design—What you need to do and When

- Build—How to best do those things

- Operate—Who is responsible for which tasks

To learn, earn, and reinvent your Enterprise better and faster, the knowledge work productivity system and principles in this book can help. In addition, a better and more practical knowledge work productivity tool is needed. Just as assembly lines help manual workers increase their productivity using fixed assets, a specialized knowledge work productivity instrument is needed to help knowledge workers become more productive and more successful as they accelerate their Enterprise projects.

The knowledge work productivity and Enterprise reinvention tool, *Strategic Profiling*®, is specially designed to help individuals, functions, and organizations make the invisible nature of knowledge work more visible and more productive. Based on the knowledge work productivity system in this book, it has been developed to help managers reinvent their Enterprises—by helping project teams accelerate their Enterprise initiatives. This tool is described in detail in the next chapter.

Chapter Nine: Capitalize on Your Enterprise Knowledge Work Landscape

"Knowing and then capitalizing on a project team's knowledge work landscape is similar to building a house. Since landscapes are unique, houses need to be designed and constructed differently as well—depending on whether they are in a dense city, in a sprawling suburb, on the beach, or in the mountains. In every Enterprise and Enterprise project there is an underlying knowledge work landscape, depending on the individuals involved. It's important to identify your unique landscape and then execute the path for Enterprise reinvention that most productively takes advantage its distinct characteristics."

Chapter Nine

CAPITALIZE ON YOUR ENTERPRISE KNOWLEDGE WORK LANDSCAPE

Manual work can be managed productively through physical mechanisms such as assembly lines and objective command and control management techniques. Knowledge work requires a productivity management tool as well. This chapter focuses on the tool and process developed in conjunction with the work in this book to help teams manage knowledge work and Enterprise reinvention better and faster. The following sections describe this in greater detail:

- Making your invisible knowledge work landscape more visible

- Creating an Enterprise knowledge work productivity profile

- Integrating the four Enterprise knowledge work subcultures

- Making your unique knowledge work profile more productive

- The *Strategic Profiling®* knowledge work productivity instrument

- Example: Applying *Strategic Profiling* to an Enterprise knowledge work project

- Reinventing your Enterprise better and faster

Making your invisible knowledge work landscape more visible

As I described in Chapter One, the sign of successful Enterprise knowledge work is when one of the following three results occurs:

- Something successful that never existed previously, is now up and running

- Something successful that existed previously has been improved or expanded

- Something unsuccessful that existed previously has been stopped

The productivity of this work can be judged by the speed with which it is achieved and the cost to finish the job. To implement projects better and faster, a tool and process is needed to help knowledge workers better understand their unique "knowledge work landscapes."

Knowing and then capitalizing on a project team's knowledge work landscape is similar to building a house. For example, to build a home, climate, population density, and terrain need to be considered. Since landscapes are unique, houses need to be designed and constructed differently as well, depending on whether they are in a dense city, in a sprawling suburb, on the beach, or in the mountains.

To improve your company's productivity, it's important to identify your unique landscape and then execute the path for reinvention—through Enterprise projects—that best fits you and your organization. The invisible nature of knowledge work needs to be made visible and then be explicitly managed using the Envision-Design-Build-Operate knowledge work productivity system. *Strategic Profiling* was developed to help companies do this.

As part of this process, it's important to factor in that people and organizations have opposing orientations. The key is to stay focused on the overarching architecture of the playing field—between knowledge, work, subjectivity, and objectivity. These opposing poles accommodate multiple personalities that need to be understood and managed. The important thing is to first make sense of them and then make them more productive. In some respects, it's similar to Mark Twain's insight that once we realize that we are all crazy life can be explained. More on this is described in the knowledge work subcultures section of this chapter.

Creating your Enterprise knowledge work productivity profile

It's useful to think about *Strategic Profiling* in the context of other survey-based instruments. Many psychologically-based surveys are available to help people turn the invisible nature of how they think into something that is more visible and actionable. Most tools are grounded in psychology and focus on understanding and managing individual preferences and differences [238]. They are excellent at improving self-awareness. A few of the surveys used in the business environment include:

- Myers-Briggs Type Indicator® [239]

- Herrmann Brain Dominance Instrument® [70]

- David Keirsey Temperament Sorter® [240]

- John Lopker Pictures of Personality® [241]

Many psychologically-based surveys match individual teaching styles with individual learning styles [238, 242-244], but none specifically focuses on improving Enterprise knowledge work productivity [245]. Even though there are some similarities between them, no unification mechanism exists either [238].

Unification is important to knowledge work because holism is a key ingredient of the work itself. It's helpful to be able to apply the same framework across multiple levels and situations. A single framework will not always be perfect, but using one is clearly more productive. In Chapter Two I described a number of similarities between sociological frameworks and the knowledge work productivity system. There are also several psychologically-based survey classification systems that are logically consistent with the Envision-Design-Build-Operate knowledge work landscape. For example:

Strategic Profiling®	Myers-Briggs®	Keirsey®	Herrmann®	Lopker®
Envision	Intuiting	Idealists	Visualizers	Clarifier
Design	Thinking	Rationals	Analyzers	Unifier
Build	Sensing	Guardians	Organizers	Stabilizer
Operate	Feeling	Artisans	Personalizers	Activator

The *Strategic Profiling* instrument was designed in conjunction with the principles in this book. So, not surprisingly, I prefer it. At the same time, given some of the similarities between instruments, if you prefer another survey tool, this chapter is written in a way that will make it easier for you to apply your favorite instrument more productively with Enterprise projects.

Strategic Profiling was developed by integrating a number of business, psychological, and sociological perspectives [9, 44, 60, 63, 67, 69, 70, 74, 77, 246] to help individuals, functions, and organizations improve their knowledge work productivity and reinvent their Enterprises better and faster. It helps make a project team's preferences, abilities, and priorities more visible so that your company's Enterprise projects can be managed more productively.

The opposing forces of knowledge, work, subjectivity, and objectivity described in this book produce fifteen different knowledge worker landscapes, or Strategic Profiles. In some surveys one profile is considered better than another. With *Strategic Profiling* every profile is equal—but unique—with respect to productivity-related strengths and weaknesses. My profile isn't better than yours, and your profile isn't better than mine. Each one has a preferred productivity path depending on its underlying characteristics. The key is to capitalize on the insights that the instrument provides to better manage and accelerate your Enterprise projects so that you can reinvent your Enterprise better and faster.

Integrating the four Enterprise knowledge work subcultures

To manage knowledge work productivity better, the four primary knowledge work subcultures (Envision-Design-Build-Operate) need to be visible, well understood, properly integrated, and productively sequenced. They need to be seen and managed as part of the overall knowledge work productivity system.

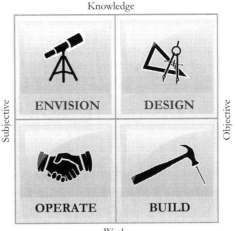

Envision: The "Envision subculture" is a society of subjective thinkers. They are the most likely to enjoy spontaneity and generating new knowledge but will generally not be energized by plans and field work. They are often great at brainstorming and seeing the possibilities. At the same time, they can resist rules and get turned off if they need to do the same things over and over again.

Design: The "Design subculture" is a society of objective thinkers. They are most likely to enjoy structured knowledge and planning but aren't inclined to like spontaneity and mingling with people. They are great at measuring performance and establishing rules. At the same time, they probably won't like surprises and will be inclined to resist small talk.

Build: The "Build subculture" is a society of objective workers. They are the most likely to enjoy field work and systematization but won't necessarily like spontaneity or adapting to changing needs. They are great at standardizing processes and using established tools. At the same time, they can be inclined to resist new ideas and be unfriendly to inexperienced people.

Operate: The "Operate subculture" is a society of subjective workers. They are the most likely to enjoy spontaneity and get energy from personal interactions but often won't enjoy things like standard procedures, reports and policies. They are likely to be great with social skills and at being opportunistic. At the same time, they may be resistant to rules and regulations.

Since knowledge work productivity is impacted by differences in abilities, preferences, and priorities, there are common dysfunctions that need to be managed within and between the Envision-Design-Build-Operate subcultures. Each subculture brings benefits and disadvantages, but when the orientations become extreme they can produce especially unproductive Enterprise dysfunctions.

Extreme Envision dysfunction: This produces too many ideas with insufficient discipline. A blind spot is often impracticality and not enough constancy of purpose. This can impair productivity by not taking full advantage of what is tested, proven, and already in place.

Extreme Design dysfunction: This produces too many decision makers (and "unmakers") and too many rules and regulations and leads to analysis paralysis. A blind spot is often an internal focus that lets perfection get in the way of sufficiency. This reduces Enterprise productivity by creating solutions that cost more than the problems they are trying to address.

Extreme Build dysfunction: This produces high internal resistance to change and encourages Enterprises and Enterprise projects to stay fully focused on what has worked in the past. A blind spot is often an internal and historically oriented focus. This can reduce productivity by systematizing too much and clutching on to the past when future success requires structural change.

Extreme Operate dysfunction: This produces conditions where no one seems to be in charge, with constant fire fighting as one of its symptoms. A blind spot is that the short term can be emphasized at the expense of the longer term. This can reduce productivity by confusing others and increasing costs through too many one-off efforts.

Making your unique knowledge work profile more productive

As explained earlier, knowing your knowledge work productivity profile, or landscape, is important to manage knowledge work more productively. The group version of the online tool described in this chapter was designed for this purpose. The individual version, on *www.StrategicProfiling.com,* is free so that people can easily apply the knowledge work productivity system at a personal level.

Strategic Profiling is not a test where certain results are better than others. It is common for people to favor their own profiles, but doing this is unproductive, especially in Enterprise project teams. It is important to view and manage these profiles as part of the larger knowledge work productivity system. Since every profile has its own pros and cons, the key is to understand and then capitalize on the most productive path for each individual-function-organization's unique landscape.

The Strategic Profiling knowledge work productivity instrument

With knowledge work, when different people have the same goals, they will commonly take different paths to reach them—based on their personal preferences, priorities, abilities, and life experiences. If this isn't proactively managed, productivity will suffer because these invisible paths are often incompatible.

Strategic Profiling is a tool to give visibility to these otherwise conflicting mental models to help people see the bigger picture and create a more productive way forward using the Envision-Design-Build-Operate system. The free personal version of *Strategic Profiling* has thirty-five questions, and the group version—focused on the individual-function-organization—has sixty-five. Each knowledge work profile has distinct advantages, disadvantages, and a unique path for increasing knowledge work productivity. I will only describe one profile as an example, but there are fifteen possible ones:

The Visionary	The Analytic Coach	The Active Visionary
The Designer	The Structured Worker	The Thinking Builder
The Builder	The Spontaneous Worker	The Active Designer
The Operator	The Enterprise Thinker	The Thinking Operator
The Strategic Organizer	The Enterprise Worker	The Holistic Worker

To give you a better sense of the Strategic Profiles that result from the survey, here is an example of one of the classifications—The Visionary. It is described as follows:

THE VISIONARY

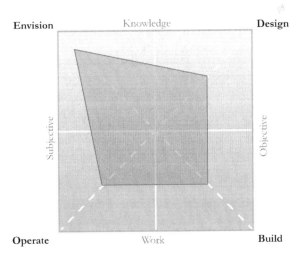

This profile emerges when there is unusual strength in the Envision work-behavior area. *The Visionary* profile—with individuals, functions, and organizations—produces a knowledge work orientation that solves problems through new and creative ideas. *The Visionary* prefers focusing on the question "Where do we intend to go and Why"?

For *The Visionary* profile to be more productive, it is important for these individuals-functions-organizations to engage other team members and use management routines to emphasize and integrate:

• What work needs to be done When

• How that work should best be done

• Who should be responsible for which tasks

If all four areas aren't integrated, *The Visionary* will be unproductive because their creative ideas will not be implemented effectively, efficiently, or sustainably.

Example: Applying Strategic Profiling to an Enterprise knowledge work project

For companies to be reinvented, Enterprise projects need to successfully integrate the objective and subjective natures of knowledge and work through Envision-Design-Build-Operate. Doing this better is at the heart of getting to benefits sooner, competing more effectively in a changing environment, and improving investment returns on the projects themselves.

To help you better visualize how the knowledge work productivity instrument can be used in practice, I will use an Enterprise technology project as an example. This is not written as a case study, but frames up specific steps so that you can more easily apply the details in this chapter to your own situation—with or without the *Strategic Profiling* instrument. An Enterprise technology project is a good illustration because these types of initiatives are often the most expensive knowledge work tasks that Enterprises undertake. They also have high problem rates using manual work project management techniques.

The Enterprise technology project example in this chapter is divided into five parts to better demonstrate how the *Strategic Profiling* tool and knowledge work productivity principles can be applied in practice:

1) The anatomy of an Enterprise technology project

2) Using the Group *Strategic Profiling* instrument to improve knowledge work visibility

3) Reviewing and reflecting on the results personally

4) Reviewing and reflecting on the results as a project team

5) Establishing a productive action plan at the operational level

Strategic Profiling Example. The anatomy of an Enterprise technology project

Large Enterprise technology projects commonly begin with high expectations, a large capital budget approval, and a detailed business case.

A variety of key players are involved—across multiple legal entities—including executive management, the program director, a consulting firm to manage the project's implementation, the software owner, and the company's board.

To manage Enterprise technology projects better, it is important to holistically understand their anatomy. Here is what the five key players are responsible for and how it all fits together:

- Executive management: recommends the project and is ultimately responsible

- Program director: runs the project for the Enterprise

- Consulting systems integrator: oversees the technical aspects of the project

- Software supplier: owns the application

- The board: approves funding and provides strategic oversight

Historically, Enterprise projects have been implemented using Scientific Management methods, and this approach has struggled or failed 70% of the time. To understand why, it's important to know how the players interact with one other from a knowledge work productivity perspective, and the problems—and red flags—that need to be managed.

First, executive management puts many of the key players in place. And the executive team is ultimately responsible for what happens. They need to ensure that Envision-Design-Build-Operate are well connected and continually in sequence. Once a project begins, however, these key managers are often quick to move on to their day-to-day responsibilities and priorities. Then, slowly but surely, the project and the company's executives become disconnected. Committees grow, they become less focused, and the project itself slows down because critical tradeoff decisions don't get made fast enough, if at all. The project then, to get the actual work done, becomes less of a business initiative and more of a technology initiative. This makes the project less productive and less successful.

Technology projects can be more productive when they are holistically linked to business-oriented master plans owned by the business executives and the board—including the Where-Why-What-When-How-Who of the knowledge work productivity system. These plans need to make sense in business terms. A common productivity red flag is when executives begin hearing technology jargon from the project team. This signals the problem that key business people have disengaged or have not productively engaged in the first place.

In large Enterprise projects, business tradeoffs need to be made early and often. This can only be done by executive management. Otherwise, consensus management will at least double or triple the cost of the project. Difficult business issues need to be solved early in the project when the energy is highest. Many Enterprise project teams make the mistake of trying to start out with all the easy decisions and hope the difficult issues will take care of themselves later. This is a common and sometimes fatal mistake.

Another key player in large Enterprise technology projects is the program director. Due to knowledge work dysfunctions, program directors have high failure rates even though they have often had very successful careers up until that point. Program directors can easily get consumed by the details of the project in the Design and Build areas without enough time to ensure that the Envision step is clear and that the Operate step is productive.

Program directors typically possess a major weakness as well as a major strength. The first scenario is when they know the company well and don't have experience managing major enterprise technology projects and large consulting systems integrators. The second situation is when they have experience with major technology projects but don't know the company and its key players well. With both scenarios the program director, and the Enterprise project itself, can benefit from independent and experienced facilitation support. This needs to be distinct from the integrator because cost overruns typically benefit the integrator. Not seeing independent and experienced support for the program director is a second knowledge work productivity red flag.

The third key player in large Enterprise technology projects is the consulting systems integrator. They are the largest vendor. Integrators are hired to bring project management, configuration, and implementation expertise to the project. They are often focused on the objective world of Design and Build. When the program director, board, and executive management get disconnected from the more subjective areas of Envision (Where the project intends to go and Why) and Operate (Who is responsible for which tasks inside and outside the project team), productivity often suffers—with consultants working on the wrong things and not held accountable for working on the right things. Systems integrators are also generally incented to sell hours and generate margin for their firms. This can create problems due to Parkinson's Law as well as agency theory problems described in Chapter Seven. It adds fuel to the natural knowledge work problem of work expanding to fill the available time. Having dysfunctional incentive architectures makes this even worse.

The knowledge work productivity red flag with the systems integrator is when the consulting firm can win while the client loses through cost overruns due to time delays or change order provisions. Also, it's a red flag when the firm can check its own work when there are problems or cost overruns. This problem benefits from independent oversight due to the decision making and incentive problems explained in Chapter Four.

A fourth key player in Enterprise technology projects is the software owner. They own the applications being installed and license their software to the client. They are the long-term strategic vendor, long after the project is implemented, because they are responsible for maintaining and enhancing the software after it goes live. A key long-term knowledge work productivity issue is when clients introduce configuration complexity that conflicts with the design of the software itself. This occurs when there are tradeoff dysfunctions, as described in Chapter Three.

The knowledge work productivity red flag with the software owner is if they do not have enough access to easily make it known when the project team is making decisions that will have bad technical repercussions. Without independent facilitation, it can often be difficult for software owners to raise these technical issues because the software owner and systems integrator are also key sources of business for one another. Thus, when there is a problem, it's hard for the software owner to ruffle the feathers of the integrator or the integrator's client.

The fifth key player in Enterprise technology projects is the board. The board has oversight responsibility for the project in that it approves funding and oversees Enterprise strategy and Enterprise risk. Typically boards only get information tied to the project's budget. Unfortunately, budgets can be very misleading because they can look good early on if the project is not progressing. They can also incorrectly look bad in the early stages if projects are doing better than the forecast. More than any other key player, because of their oversight role, the board needs an independent and holistic picture of where the project has been, where it is currently, and where it needs to go next—in the context of the Enterprise's vision.

The knowledge work productivity red flag here is when the board only sees Enterprise projects being managed by budgets and does not see an independent and Enterprise-level contingency process in place. An independent contingency process is needed for all key players, and especially the board, to holistically identify and manage risk factors before they become major problems. Compared to a financial budget, contingency management offers a much broader and longer view of a project—focused on productively managing the risks associated with schedule, budget, quality and effectiveness, and overall scope. A resource that is independent from the systems integrator, software owner, and even the external auditor is important so that there are no real or perceived conflicts of interest.

These five Enterprise project red flags are often missed until it's too late. Since knowledge work is invisible, it's important to use a tool—in the context of this holistic anatomy and these red flags—to increase visibility and help project teams properly apply the knowledge work productivity system. The *Strategic Profiling* instrument and the following process were designed for this purpose.

Example. Step One: Using the Group "Strategic Profiling" instrument

The first step of the Group *Strategic Profiling* process is for each member of the Enterprise project team to personally and confidentially complete the sixty-five question survey. This generally takes twenty to forty minutes and in conjunction with a one-day working session can save months of unproductive effort. The survey itself should be done with a specific Enterprise project in mind.

The Group *Strategic Profiling* instrument is designed to capture and integrate important knowledge work productivity factors. For example, one characteristic is "Making Decisions by the Numbers." On this factor, the survey asks the team members to individually rate the characteristic as either excellent, above average, average, below average, or poor—for the individual, the functional group, and the organization overall. The tool also asks team members to describe their preference and priority—from strong agreement to strong disagreement—with respect to whether the individual enjoys "making decisions by the numbers." In addition, the survey inquires as to whether the person thinks the function should place more emphasis on "making decisions by the numbers." In *Strategic Profiling* this is done for twenty-eight key knowledge work productivity characteristics.

Example. Step Two: Reviewing and reflecting on the results personally

As soon as every individual in the project team has completed their online survey, each person is sent a personal and confidential report electronically. The next step is for each individual to review and reflect on their own document for about an hour, prior to meeting as a group. Individual reports are designed to help team members understand themselves and their group better through the Envision-Design-Build-Operate lens.

The personalized knowledge work productivity landscape analysis provides sixteen key considerations for individuals to reflect on.

Strategic Profiling® Report Sixteen Reflection Points
Individual Reflection at the Personal Level (Using a five point scale)
1. How the individual rates his or her personal abilities and preferences
2. The individual's most favorite knowledge work characteristics
3. The individual's least favorite knowledge work characteristics
4. The individual's Strategic Profile based on preferences and abilities
5. Individual assessment of their function's and organization's knowledge work abilities
6. How the individual views the function's and organization's knowledge work strengths
7. Individual view of the function's and organization's knowledge work weaknesses
8. The individual's perception of the functional and organizational Strategic Profile
9. Personal view on knowledge work characteristics that the function emphasizes
Individual Reflection on the Group (Using a five point scale)
10. Group scores for functional and organizational knowledge work abilities
11. Group scores for functional and organizational knowledge work strengths
12. Group scores for functional and organizational knowledge work weaknesses
13. Group perception of the functional and organizational Strategic Profiles
14. The ten largest knowledge work misconceptions
15. Group view on what the function emphasizes from a knowledge work perspective
16. Group's perceived and actual Strategic Profiles

In the *Strategic Profiling* report, knowledge work "ability" characteristics are scored on a five-point scale: Excellent, Above Average, Average, Below Average, or Extremely Poor. "Preferences" are also scored on a five-point scale based on enjoyment of each characteristic using Strongly Agree, Agree, Neutral, Disagree, and Strongly Disagree statements. "Priorities" are scored based on the emphasis that the function/group places on each knowledge work characteristic.

All sixteen knowledge work reflection points, for different reasons, are important to individually understand and digest after the *Strategic Profiling* survey has been completed. By personally understanding and reflecting on the instrument's results, steps three and four of the group process will be much more productive.

Example. Step Three: Reflecting on the results as a project team

The third step of the *Strategic Profiling* process is for the project team to review and discuss the combined results of the group survey. This is important so that team members can improve their personal understanding of the knowledge work productivity system in the context of their unique group, organization, and Enterprise project.

This step, consistent with Drucker's philosophy, focuses on the group's task at hand. It is important to get the project team on the same page so that they can co-create a shared Enterprise view and a productive game plan to achieve better and faster results. You may remember that manual work focuses on the right answers whereas knowledge work needs to concentrate on the right questions. Therefore, it is important for the group to get clear on asking and answering at a high level the four primary knowledge work productivity questions:

1) Envision—Where do we intend to go and Why?

2) Design—What needs to happen and When?

3) Build—How can we best do those things?

4) Operate—Who should be responsible for which tasks?

This will happen much faster if everyone writes down their answers first and then discusses them as a group with a facilitator and a decision maker. Once this is done, it's important to individually and collectively ask and answer four more questions, linked to the Enterprise project being undertaken:

1) What is your greatest hope?

2) What is your greatest fear?

3) What is the biggest individual-functional-organizational barrier?

4) What is the greatest individual-functional-organizational asset?

Once this has been addressed by each individual within the group, it's important to then discuss the *Strategic Profiling* results as a group. Through this step the project team can better understand their unique knowledge work landscape and determine the most productive way to move forward with their Enterprise project. The Group Summary report has the following sections:

Strategic Profiling® Group Summary Sections:
1) Function / Project Team and Organizational highlights
2) Functional strengths
3) Organizational strengths
4) Functional weaknesses
5) Organizational weaknesses
6) Key misconceptions on abilities
7) Areas that receive too much emphasis
8) Areas that may not receive enough emphasis
9) Perceived Strategic Profile of the Function and Organization
10) Actual Strategic Profile of the Function
11) Most productive path for the Function
12) Discussion on areas that may not receive enough emphasis
13) Discussion on harnessing the strengths and weaknesses of the team
14) Discussion on what one thing needs to change most
15) Discussion on what one thing needs to stay the same

Example. Step Four: Developing a productive action plan

Developing a productive project game plan is the final Group *Strategic Profiling* step. By now the team will be familiar with the anatomy of their knowledge work project, will have completed the survey, reviewed and reflected upon their results, and been involved in a group discussion on their knowledge work landscape and the Enterprise project itself. Now, it is important to reconsider the four primary knowledge work productivity questions through an operational lens. The higher-level answers in step three can now be refined in the context of an action plan that is specific, measurable, achievable, realistic, and time bound.

The project team should now readdress the four primary knowledge work productivity questions with a single deadline in mind. Similar to before, it will be much more productive if they are answered individually before they are discussed as a group. Once the shared timeframe is clear, the following questions should be re-asked, re-answered, and integrated into a productive game plan:

1) Envision—Where do we intend to go and Why?

2) Design—What needs to happen and When?

3) Build—How can we best do those things?

4) Operate—Who will be responsible for which tasks?

When these questions were answered at a high level in step three, it wasn't necessary to have a single time frame because it was more important for the individuals and the group to create a united story—in their own minds and as a group—with general agreement on Where-Why-What-When-How-Who. In step three, different time frames will be common. For example, Envision will often have a longer time frame than Design. In step four, however, this needs to become more operational. Depending on the project, this time frame should be no more than a year and is often best if it is a defined number of months or even weeks. The meeting's ultimate decision-maker may need to make a decision on the single time frame based on various inputs from the group. This step closes the loop—to more productively get an Enterprise project moving forward in an accelerated and sustainable way.

To summarize, the *Strategic Profiling* process for accelerated Enterprise projects first requires a common understanding of the anatomy of the project itself, including red flags to look out for. Next, the individuals of the project team need to complete the group version of the *Strategic Profiling* instrument. This takes twenty to forty minutes. Third, they should reflect on their confidential *Strategic Profiling* report for about an hour. Fourth, it is important to discuss their project as a group. Finally, a clear action plan needs to be developed and articulated—linked to the knowledge work productivity system and a specific timeframe. This can usually be done in a single day. Investing this day will save a significant amount of time and money during the life of the Enterprise project.

Reinventing your Enterprise better and faster

Making your individual-functional-organizational knowledge work landscape more visible will help you accelerate your Enterprise projects and reinvent your Enterprise faster and on a more sustainable basis.

The importance of this reinvention for many companies cannot be overstated because of the challenges they face and the fact that the management methods that worked so well in the 20th century have clearly become constrained. To create a brighter future in the Knowledge Age, we need to reinvent our Enterprises and move forward with the next frontier of management, focused on improving knowledge work productivity.

There has never been a better time to reinvent your Enterprise. This is the subject of the next and final chapter.

Chapter Ten: Reinvent Your Enterprise Today

"Reinventing Enterprises through a knowledge work productivity lens is important work. While traditional companies have enjoyed many successes over the years, in the Knowledge Age they will no longer be able to try being better caterpillars every year or tighten their belts one more time. A step-change in sustainable performance requires Enterprise reinvention, and Enterprise reinvention depends on better knowledge work productivity."

Chapter Ten

REINVENT YOUR ENTERPRISE TODAY

Enterprise reinvention through better knowledge work productivity is the most important management challenge of the 21st century. This is true for companies and institutions, and has profound implications for our society overall.

It's clear that every management system can take us only so far before it becomes constrained. The same approach that improved manual work productivity in the 20th century now constrains knowledge work productivity in the 21st century. Specialized knowledge work principles and tools are required to overcome the productivity paradox that haunts many established companies today.

Our management challenge is to transcend Scientific Management despite its success in the 20th century. It's time to move from scientific manual work management toward cybernetic knowledge work management—consistent with the ideas of Peter Drucker, Norbert Wiener, Talcott Parsons, Gibson Burrell, and Gareth Morgan. If we are successful and can improve knowledge work productivity as our predecessors increased manual work productivity, we are at the threshold of an unparalleled economic expansion. If not, Drucker was right to warn us that our economic prosperity is at risk.

Enterprises must reinvent themselves. In the same sense that a butterfly is much more than an improved caterpillar, we must do more than improve our Enterprises incrementally. To reinvent *your* Enterprise it will require metamorphosis, by successfully making the transition from a manual work mindset to one focused on managing knowledge work more productively.

For consistency, since I have woven several beverage industry examples throughout this book, I will finish with how many of the ideas in this book can be applied to *that* industry. This is an isolated illustration. Most industries need to be reinvented. This example is simply intended to provide you with some thought starters for *your* company and *your* particular industry.

Reinvention example: Beverage industry metamorphosis

The beverage industry, similar to many well-established industries in the 21st century, began during or before Frederick Taylor's Scientific Management era. Key players typically own many fixed assets, have distinct geographic territories, and have a long history with a broad base of customers and consumers. The industry was well served by Scientific Management in the 20th century, and this is true with soft drinks, juice, beer, wine, and spirits.

Today, a convergence of forces—linked to the ever-changing nature of knowledge work—pressures this industry in the same way that it challenges many others. Consolidating customers, fragmenting consumer tastes, a rapidly changing public affairs climate, and lower barriers to entry have created pressures that are difficult to navigate. So, it's useful to ask what might Enterprise reinvention mean in an industry like this?

Enterprise reinvention requires a holistic set of changes, including those related to corporate strategy, innovation, consolidation, and infrastructure management. It promises to be *most* productive when it is linked to the knowledge work productivity system itself:

- ENVISION: Reinventing Corporate Strategy and Corporate Affairs

- DESIGN: Reinventing Product Innovation

- BUILD: Reinventing Distribution, Fixed Assets, and Infrastructure

- OPERATE: Reinventing Alliances

ENVISION: Reinventing Corporate Strategy and Corporate Affairs

Historically, large beverage companies have used analytic tools to focus on well-defined markets and competitors as a key part of their corporate strategy development process. They have also typically considered corporate affairs as "the back shop," used to respond as needed to issues related to regulation and public opinion. This worked well in the Scientific Management era.

However, in the 21st century, the growth of Internet communities and Web-based communication vehicles has created a 24/7 platform for hundreds of millions of people. Cable began to change the world, but it was only the tip of the iceberg. And, a small tip at that.

In the Knowledge Age, the Corporate Affairs function can no longer be seen as the back shop, just as strategy can no longer be an analytic exercise around well-defined markets and competitors. Corporate Affairs in most industries now needs to be the lens through which companies view their markets and construct and execute their corporate strategy.

Your Enterprise is indeed your corporate brand in the Knowledge Age. As politically, socially, and commercially oriented communities continue to blend, for companies to reinvent themselves, a more commercially oriented Corporate Affairs lens is needed to define markets, position competitors, and increase economic performance.

Implementing a community-based corporate strategy will require a significant change for many beverage companies. Nonetheless, using Corporate Affairs as the lens for corporate reinvention will help create a common denominator for organizations and their ecosystems—including corporate strategy, consumer positioning, legal affairs, industry associations, community involvement, employee communications, investor relations, government affairs, and media relations.

Reinvention will be difficult if companies think of their Corporate Affairs function in historic and specialized terms as a communication vehicle for political and media constituencies. Corporate Affairs will increasingly need to be the lens through which companies innovate and market their products and services with consumers and customers.

DESIGN: Reinventing Product Innovation

As with other industries, the best way for the beverage industry to reinvent itself is to innovate with consumers and customers. Historically, Scientific Management helped develop the profitable mass market. Now, the challenge is to profitably develop the tailored market. This is an important shift. To describe further, in the beverage industry sales historically could be represented by a normal curve—where a few well-known and consistently growing products produced high volumes and high profits. The market has shifted toward a bimodal sales curve, where mass marketers now face simultaneous pressures on both ends of the spectrum. Their high-volume products are getting pressure on price, and new low-volume products are being rapidly introduced by niche competitors.

This is a challenging shift for many established consumer products companies because it simultaneously puts gross profit pressure on established brands and requires disproportionate capital investment for newer products. Although new products can generate higher gross margins per sale, they have riskier long-term economic returns and have so far resulted in a disappointing track record of "one-year-wonders." Many new products are introduced with great fanfare and then discontinued within three years. This makes innovating with customers the safest and most productive way to innovate—versus an internally-focused laboratory mindset.

Innovation is important. But, it needs to be *productive* innovation created with customers. The bimodal market shift has put large beverage companies—similar to many other established firms—in a difficult growth and profit position. Simply putting a larger number of new products through traditional pipelines is not productive innovation. Without changing the underlying Enterprise structure, it is not sustainable.

An additional complication for established companies is that as they focus more on niche products and line extensions, it puts more pressure on their traditional product and asset bases. As I described in Chapter Three, this problem is something that Sam Ginn masterfully managed when he created AirTouch within Pacific Telesis and then spun it off so that it could spread its wings.

Sustainable innovation will require systemic innovation with customers using a clear product and service menu to better manage markets, brands, packages, and infrastructure as a total system. As noted in Chapter Four, with the explosion of new products and services, companies and industries will need to productively innovate and reinvent their infrastructures as part of their product and service menu designs.

BUILD: *Reinventing Distribution, Fixed Assets, and Infrastructure*

Reinventing your Enterprise requires, as Drucker emphasized, organized abandonment of the past and direct reinvestment in the future. This can be made more productive by using financial valuation principles to rethink asset management (Chapter Seven). To repeat, accelerated growth creates the most value, sustainable operating income improvement places second, and one-time cost reductions and fixed assets generate the least value.

Much of the beverage industry has consolidated aggressively over the past few decades. By now it has become clear that too much time and money have been spent consolidating old structures, with not enough time and money invested in designing and implementing alternative structures.

A key question that traditional companies will need to reflect on and answer from a knowledge work perspective is why so many fixed assets still need to be directly owned and managed. Especially since fixed assets create the least amount of value for the firms. In the 21st century market, it will not be sustainable for beverage companies to own and manage fixed assets the same way they did in the 19th and 20th centuries. A fixed-asset-less mindset should be the starting point for rethinking and reinventing beverage companies and the beverage industry overall.

Geographically based digital integration, using much of the same technology that is the basis for Google Maps and other geo-based tools, is the most practical and sustainable way for industries to rationalize the disintegrated nature of many companies and other franchised systems in the Knowledge Age. Digital integration can be achieved at a fraction of the cost of an acquisition and produce a multiple of the benefits. This too will work best if it's designed through the Corporate Affairs lens described earlier.

The beverage industry has accumulated billions of dollars of fixed assets but is not in the fixed asset management business. To reinvent itself, the industry will need to consider changing its thinking in this regard and not invest time and money trying to get better at something it shouldn't be doing at all. A more focused third party with the right skills and capital structure will prove to be a better option in the Knowledge Age. This transition to an asset-less knowledge work mindset is needed to achieve greater market focus from executives and better asset management by professional fixed asset managers.

OPERATE: Reinventing Alliances

One of the most difficult yet important tasks for beverage industry reinvention will be its ability to strategically and holistically reposition core functions internally and transition non-core functions to external partners. This will require strong relationships, productive alliances, and long attention spans.

Done properly, outsourcing is not a dirty word. It also should not be seen purely as a cost-cutting measure. And doing it piecemeal is very unproductive because the whole—not the parts—needs to be optimized. As with fixed assets, it's important to ask and answer the question, "Where do companies own their non-core processes and where do non-core processes own them by demanding too much valuable management time?" Similar to other industries, key functions to rethink include accounting processes, information technology infrastructure, logistics infrastructure, human resources administration, and indirect procurement. Done properly this should be one step of many in this direction.

Outsourcing should be done in a way that benefits your core business and your core team through better focus. This is a strategic knowledge work productivity issue. If it's not addressed as such, beverage and other companies will increasingly find that they are unable to concentrate enough on building value with their customers because their non-core activities and fragmented alliances are creating too much of a management distraction.

The beverage industry reinvention prescription

Similar to many industries and companies, where success in the past depended on internal capabilities in the manual work world, future success will require a combination of internal and external capabilities in the Knowledge Age. In the 21st century it will be necessary to move beyond the system that worked so well in the 20th century but has increasingly turned into a business constraint. The future will belong to those who:

- Define their strategy through a Corporate Affairs lens

- Innovate their infrastructure and their product line through a product and service menu

- Digitally integrate rather than legally consolidate

- Rethink fixed-asset management

- Strategically and holistically rethink core and non-core functions

While traditional companies have enjoyed many successes, in the Knowledge Age they will no longer be able to try being better caterpillars every year or tighten their belts one more time. A step-change in sustainable performance will require Enterprise reinvention.

Reinventing your Enterprise begins and ends with your customers

To win on a sustainable basis, your Enterprise needs to reinvent itself with your customers. In the process, you will receive from your customers—in more or less direct proportion—what you provide them. If you and your team can productively help your customers lower their costs and be more successful, your Enterprise will also become more successful.

A key to successful and sustainable Enterprise reinvention is to continually build and improve your Enterprise capabilities and extend your distinct advantages to a growing base of clients. As I described in Chapter Four, this requires linking your Enterprise's intellectual property to a clearly focused product and service menu.

As part of this effort, place your Enterprise signature on every customer interaction. Your Enterprise is your corporate brand. The way you serve your customers needs to consistently reinforce who you are, what you do, and how you do it. It is therefore important to systematically understand your client's environment and business problems, work with your customers to establish a winning vision, and design a practical approach with clear steps.

Over time, your Enterprise can only be successful as a firm if you can help your clients achieve their goals better and faster. Your company will need to consistently exceed customer expectations, show a genuine interest in people, act with integrity, communicate with clarity, and earn a reputation for individual and firm expertise. The knowledge work productivity system described in this book can help Enterprises manage this better because it establishes a sequential thought process to help solve client problems better, faster, and less expensively. All four steps—Envision-Design-Build-Operate—are needed.

Enthusiastic clients who are getting an excellent return on their investment with you will be central to your sustainable competitive advantage. Since building a strong client relationship takes time, and losing a customer can occur in an instant, relationships are ultimately the most critical assets that companies create. Some winning considerations as you reinvent your Enterprise with your customers are:

- The world belongs to the simplifiers and the clarifiers.

- Continually raise your awareness so that clients think of you first.

- Look for important opportunities that are difficult for clients to address internally.

- Remember that trust, credibility, and results are the basis of strong client relationships.

- If your customer likes your people, they will love your company.

- Genuine commitment and passion ultimately win customers.

To reinvent your Enterprise, first build trust through character, competence, a coherent vision, and rational programs to attain goals. Next, earn respect and become well liked by the leaders and non-leaders of your customer's organization—don't just focus on the economic buyers. Finally, remember that comfort is what ultimately keeps clients. This comes from consistently meeting and exceeding expectations, showing a genuine interest in people, acting with integrity, communicating with clarity, and having a familiar name, and respected expertise.

Reinventing your Enterprise depends on you

I will close this book where I started—with Peter Drucker. He made it clear that improving knowledge work productivity is our greatest management challenge of the 21st century. It is also at the heart of sustainable Enterprise reinvention.

In your particular organization, Enterprise reinvention is in *your* hands. As you reinvent *your* Enterprise, it will be important to create a clear and consistent story. Don't only tell what is going on but also show what it means. Follow the knowledge work productivity system: Where you intend to go and Why, What needs to happen and When, How to best proceed, and Who is responsible for which tasks.

Reinvention will begin and end with your customers. Be more professional, more experienced, and have a clearer vision than your competitors. While it is important to have a clear plan, it is also important to be open to a better alternative if an unplanned opportunity emerges—but continually keep Envision, Design, Build, and Operate connected and balanced. Link every change to your original storyline, continually reinforcing your vision for the Enterprise:

- Keep your communications crisp but flowing.

- Listen more than you speak.

- Ask questions more than you make statements.

- Remember that it's not just what you say, it's also how you say it.

- Communicate with headlines and connect the dots so that others don't need to.

For knowledge work to be productive, bonding is also important to improve chemistry and help your people produce more as a team than they can produce as individuals. To achieve this on a sustainable basis, there are a few important knowledge work productivity accelerators to keep in mind:

- Have a clear goal and a clear plan—uncertainty undermines teamwork.

- Accept and embrace the fact that everyone is different—success will not come from changing people to be more like you.

- Focus and channel the diversity of your team using the knowledge work productivity system.

- Frequently take your team's temperature to maintain morale and continually discuss what is going well and what could be going better.

- Create opportunities to spend time together, even if this means simply working together or being on a joint conference call.

- Celebrate successes and reward the contributions of others.

- Share your load with others, just as others share their load with you.

The time is right for continuous reinvention. During the 20th century, manual work productivity improvements generated previously unthinkable levels of prosperity for many people. Today, as individuals, Enterprises, and societies, we are, in Author Bob Buford's parlance, at the "halftime" [247, 248]. Our predecessors made major contributions in the 20th century, but we are temporarily stuck. In the 21st century our challenge is to build upon the achievements of those before us and become more successful *and* more significant—forging ahead with the next frontier of management. The 21st century is a new half and, for all practical purposes, a brand new game.

We live at a very challenging yet exciting time. Yes, there has never been so much to lose. Yet, there has also never been so much to gain. The good news is that better knowledge work productivity management can help. It can help you achieve better performance *from* your company, build more fun *into* your company, and ultimately create a better society for all.

Reinvention is the key—for you, your team, and your company. Begin Reinventing *Your* Enterprise today!

ACKNOWLEDGEMENTS

I am grateful to many people. First, I'd like to thank my family. My wife Joy, son Ted, and daughter Rachel made this book possible over a period of many years by providing me my most cherished lifelines. In addition, my parents Vernon and Evelyn Bergstrand gave me such a wonderful foundation—both are my heroes.

This book would also not have been possible without the Brand Velocity team. I deeply appreciate and respect their resiliency, and know that prototyping the company based on knowledge work principles has often been unorthodox for all of us. As part of this equation, our existence as a firm would not have been possible without our clients. If there were the equivalent to a Brand Velocity Hall of Fame, it would include Bill Casey, Michael Brewer, Alan Kisling, Bill Hartman, and Lisa Kelly from Brand Velocity. It would also include two important mentor-customers, Shaun Higgins and Bob Guido.

With respect to actually writing this book I am deeply indebted to my editor and writing coach, Cliff Carle. His Zen Master label holds true. There is no question in my mind that without his coaching this book would never have moved from my head, notes, and reference materials, into a cohesive form. Cliff made this book much better than it would have otherwise been and seemed to effortlessly get me to work harder than I had ever envisioned.

Finally, Dr. Ozgur Ekmekci, from The George Washington University, played a significant role. He helped tremendously as the *Strategic Profiling* tool was developed, and his skills in the social sciences, business, quantitative methods, and qualitative methods helped me make the instrument, as well as the book, academically sound yet actionable in practice.

BIBLIOGRAPHY

1. Drucker, P.F., *Post-capitalist society*. 1st ed. 1993, New York, NY: HarperBusiness. 232 p.

2. Drucker, P.F., *The age of discontinuity; guidelines to our changing society*. [1st ed. 1969, New York: Harper & Row. xiii, 394 p.

3. Drucker, P.F., *Knowledge-worker productivity: the biggest challenge*. California Management Review, 1999. 41(2): p. 79–94.

4. Drucker, P.F., *The future has already happened*. The Futurist, 1998. 32(8): p. 16–18.

5. Drucker, P.F., *Managing in the next society*. 1st ed. 2002, New York: St. Martin's Press. xiii, 321 p.

6. Davenport, T.H. *Was Drucker wrong?* Babsonknowledge.org 2005 [cited 05/03/2008]; Available from: http://www.babsonknowledge.org/2005/12/was_drucker_wrong.htm.

7. Senge, P.M., *The fifth discipline: the art and practice of the learning organization*. Rev. and updated. ed. 2006, New York: Doubleday/Currency. xviii, 445 p.

8. Davenport, T.H., *Thinking for a living: how to get better performance and results from knowledge workers*. 2005, Boston, Mass.: Harvard Business School Press. ix, 226 p.

9. Schwandt, D.R. and M.J. Marquardt, *Organizational learning: from world-class theories to global best practices*. 2000, Boca Raton, Fla.: St. Lucie Press. xviii, 258 p.

10. Bartlett, J.W., *Fundamentals of venture capital.* 1999, Lanham, Md.: Madison Books. viii, 165 p.

11. Gladstone, D. and L. Gladstone, *Venture capital handbook : an entrepreneur's guide to raising venture capital.* Updated and rev. ed. 2002, Upper Saddle River, NJ: Prentice Hall. xxi, 424 p.

12. Quindlen, R., *Confessions of a venture capitalist: inside the high-stakes world of start-up financing.* 2000, New York: Warner Books. xxi, 218 p.

13. Lewis, M., *The new new thing: a Silicon Valley story.* 1st ed. 2000, New York: W. W. Norton. 268 p.

14. Kawasaki, G., *The art of the start: the time-tested, battle-hardened guide for anyone starting anything.* 2004, New York: Portfolio. xii, 226 p.

15. Dewey, J., *Democracy and education.* The Barnes & Noble library of essential reading. 2005, New York: Barnes & Noble Books. xix, 420 p.

16. *Wall Street Journal Forecasting Survey for 2007*, in *Wall Street Journal.* 2007: New York. p. A2.

17. Jaques, E., *Requisite organization : a total system for effective managerial organization and managerial leadership for the 21st century.* Rev. 2nd ed. 1996, Arlington, VA: Cason Hall. 137, [12] p.

18. Jaques, E. and K. Cason, *Human capability : a study of individual potential and its application.* 1994, Falls Church, VA: Cason Hall & Co. xvi, 165 p.

19. Goldratt, E.M. and J. Cox, *The goal : excellence in manufacturing.* 1984, Croton-on-Hudson, N.Y.: North River Press. 262 p.

20. Copeland, T.E., T. Koller, and J. Murrin, *Valuation : measuring and managing the value of companies*. 3rd ed. Wiley frontiers in finance. 2000, New York: Wiley. xvi, 490 p.

21. Taylor, F.W., *The principles of scientific management*. 1st ed. 2007, Jackson Hole, WY: Archeion Press, LLC.

22. Smith, A. and E. Cannan, *The wealth of nations*. 2000, New York: Modern Library. xxvi, 1154 p.

23. Smith, A., *The wealth of nations*. 1933, London, New York: J. M. Dent & sons E. P. Dutton & co. 2 v.

24. Einstein, A. and C. Seelig, *Ideas and opinions*. 3rd ed. 1995, New York: Crown Trade Paperbacks. 377 p.

25. Senge, P.M., *The Fifth discipline fieldbook : strategies and tools for building a learning organization*. 1994, New York: Currency, Doubleday. xiii, 593 p.

26. Goldratt, E.M., *What is this thing called theory of constraints and how should it be implemented?* 1990, Croton-on-Hudson, N.Y.: North River Press. x, 162 p.

27. Kuhn, T.S., *The structure of scientific revolutions*. 3rd ed. 1996, Chicago, IL: University of Chicago Press. xiv, 212 p.

28. Pirsig, R.M., *Zen and the art of motorcycle maintenance : an inquiry into values*. Quill ed. 1999, New York: W. Morrow. 436 p.

29. Sieden, L.S., *Buckminster Fuller's universe*. 2000, Cambridge, Mass.: Perseus Pub. xviii, 510 p.

30. Rouse, W.B., *Enterprise transformation : understanding and enabling fundamental change*. 2006, Hoboken, N.J.: Wiley-Interscience. xxxii, 527 p.

31. Barnard, C.I., *The functions of the executive.* 1968, Cambridge,: Harvard University Press. xxxvi, 334 p.

32. Wright, F.L., et al., *Frank Lloyd Wright and the living city.* 1998, Weil am Rhein, Germany Milan, Italy: Vitra Design Museum; Skira. 334 p.

33. Norman, D.A., *The design of everyday things.* 1st Basic paperback. ed. 2002, New York: Basic Books. xxi, 257 p.

34. Drucker, P.F., *Managing for results : economic tasks and risk-taking decisions.* 1st Perennial Library ed. 1986, New York: Perennial Library. xiv, 240 p.

35. Drucker, P.F., *Innovation and entrepreneurship : practice and principles.* 1st ed. 1985, New York: Harper & Row. ix, 277 p.

36. Peter, L.J., *Why things go wrong, or, The Peter Principle revisited.* 1st ed. 1985, New York: W. Morrow. 207 p.

37. Parkinson, C.N., *Parkinson's law, and other studies in administration.* 1957, Boston: Houghton Mifflin. 112 p.

38. Drucker, P.F., *Knowledge work.* Executive Excellence, 2002. 19(10): p. 12.

39. Drucker, P.F., *Peter Drucker on the profession of management,* ed. N. Stone. 1998, Boston, MA: Harvard Business School Press. 224.

40. Waterman, R.H., *Adhocracy : the power to change.* The Larger agenda series,. 1990, Knoxville, Tenn.: Whittle Direct Books. 86 p.

41. Hill, N., *The law of success.* 1997, Northbrook, IL: Napoleon Hill Foundation. 1 v. (various pagings).

42. Drucker, P.F., *The new meaning of corporate social responsibility.* California Management Review, 1984. 26(2): p. 53–63.

43. Drucker, P.F., *The pension fund revolution*. [Transaction ed. 1996, New Brunswick, N.J.: Transaction Publishers. ix, 232 p.

44. Kolb, D.A., *Experiential learning : experience as the source of learning and development*. 1984, Englewood Cliffs, N.J.: Prentice-Hall. xiii, 256 p.

45. Marquardt, M.J., *Action learning in action : transforming problems and people for world-class organizational learning*. 1st ed. 1999, Palo Alto, Calif.[Alexandria, Va.]: Davies-Black Pub.; American Society for Training and Development. xviii, 259 p.

46. Merriam, S.B., R.S. Caffarella, and L. Baumgartner, *Learning in adulthood : a comprehensive guide*. 3rd ed. The Jossey-Bass higher and adult education series. 2007, San Francisco: Jossey-Bass. xvi, 533 p.

47. Schön, D.A., *Educating the reflective practitioner : toward a new design for teaching and learning in the professions*. 1st ed. The Jossey-Bass higher education series. 1987, San Francisco: Jossey-Bass. xvii, 355 p.

48. Wheatley, M.J., *Leadership and the new science : learning about organization from an orderly universe*. 1st ed. 1992, San Francisco: Berrett-Koehler Publishers. xvi, 164 p.

49. Buffett, W. and J. Lowe, *Warren Buffett speaks : wit and wisdom from the world's greatest investor*. Completely rev. and updated. ed. 2007, Hoboken, N.J.: John Wiley & Sons. xiii, 272 p.

50. Hagstrom, R.G., *The Warren Buffett way : investment strategies of the world's greatest investor*. Updated ed. 1995, New York: J. Wiley. xiv, 313 p.

51. Forbes Inc., *Forbes richest people : the Forbes annual profile of the world's wealthiest men and women*. 2007, John Wiley & Sons: New York. p. v.

52. Bell, D., *The coming of post-industrial society; a venture in social forecasting*. 1973, New York,: Basic Books. xiii, 507 p.

53. Frankl, V.E., *Man's search for meaning*. 2006, Boston: Beacon Press. xvi, 165 p.

54. McGregor, J.D., *Complexity, it's in the mind of the beholder.* Journal of Object Technology, 2006. 5(1): p. 31–37.

55. Turchin, V.F., *The phenomenon of science*. 1977, New York: Columbia University Press. xvii, 348 p.

56. O'Gorman, J.F., *ABC of architecture*. 1998, Philadelphia, Pa.: University of Pennsylvnia Press. xii, 127 p.

57. Cook, M.A., *Building enterprise information architectures : reengineering information systems*. Hewlett-Packard professional books. 1996, Upper Saddle River, NJ: Prentice Hall. xxiii, 193 p.

58. Cortada, J.W., *Best practices in information technology : how corporations get the most value from exploiting their digital investments*. 1998, Upper Saddle River, NJ: Prentice Hall PTR. xx, 250 p.

59. Forrester, J.W., *Principes des systèmes*. 3ème éd. ed. 1984, Lyon: Presses universitaires de Lyon. 1 v. (various pagings).

60. Burrell, G. and G. Morgan, *Sociological paradigms and organisational analysis : elements of the sociology of corporate life*. 1979, London: Heinemann. xiv, 432 p.

61. Weick, K.E., *The social psychology of organizing*. 2d ed. 1979, Reading, Mass.: Addison-Wesley Pub. Co. ix, 294 p.

62. Weisbord, M.R., *Productive workplaces revisited : dignity, meaning, and community in the 21st century*. [2nd ed. 2004, San Francisco: Jossey-Bass.

63. Katz, D. and R.L. Kahn, *The social psychology of organizations*. 2d ed. 1978, New York: Wiley. vi, 838 p.

64. Halbwachs, M. and L.A. Coser, *On collective memory*. The Heritage of sociology. 1992, Chicago: University of Chicago Press. 244 p.

65. Krames, J.A., *Inside Drucker's brain*. 2008, New York: Portfolio. viii, 278 p.

66. Zald, M.N., *More fragmentation? Unfinished business in linking the social sciences and the humanities*. Administrative Science Quarterly, 1996. 41: p. 251–261.

67. Jung, C.G., *Psychological types*. A revision / ed. Bollingen series. 1976, Princeton, N.J.: Princeton University Press. xv, 608 p.

68. Myers, I.B. and P.B. Myers, *Gifts differing : understanding personality type*. 1995, Palo Alto, Calif.: Davies-Black Pub.

69. Herrmann, N., *The creative brain*. 1st ed. 1988, Lake Lure, NC: Brain Books. xix, 456 p.

70. Herrmann, N., *The whole brain business book*. 1996, New York: McGraw-Hill. xvi, 334 p.

71. Jung, C.G., *Four archetypes; mother, rebirth, spirit, trickster*. 1972, London,: Routledge and K. Paul. viii, 173 p.

72. Lawrence, G., *Looking at type and learning styles*. Looking at type series. 1997, Gainesville, Fla.: CAPT, Center for Applications of Psychological Type. v, 56 p.

73. Myers, I.B. and P.B. Myers, *Gifts differing*. 10th anniversary ed. 1990, Palo Alto, CA: Consulting Psychologists Press. xxvii, 224 p.

74. Parsons, T. and E. Shils, *Toward a general theory of action*. 1951, Cambridge, MA: Harvard University Press.

75. Bluth, B.J., *Parsons' general theory of action : a summary of the basic theory*. 1982, Granada Hills, Calif.: NBS. 131 p., 9 folded leaves of plates.

76. Wiener, N., *The human use of human beings : cybernetics and society*. The Da Capo series in science. 1988, New York, N.Y.: Da Capo Press. 199 p.

77. Parsons, T., *The structure of social action* 1937, New York, NY: McGraw Hill.

78. Parsons, T., R.F. Bales, and E. Shils, *Working papers in the theory of action*. 1953, Glenco, IL: Free Press. 269 p.

79. Parsons, T., *Action theory and the human condition*. 1978, New York: Free Press. xi, 464 p.

80. Rescher, N., *Process metaphysics : an introduction to process philosophy*. SUNY series in philosophy. 1996, Albany: State University of New York Press. vii, 213 p.

81. Whitehead, A.N., D.R. Griffin, and D.W. Sherburne, *Process and reality : an essay in cosmology*. Corrected ed. Gifford lectures. 1978, New York: Free Press. xxxi, 413 p.

82. Denver, J., *Rocky Mountain High*, in *Roacky Mountain High*. 1973, RCA Records.

83. Gates, B. and C. Hemingway, *Business @ the speed of thought : using a digital nervous system*. 1999, New York, NY: Warner Books. xxii, 470 p.

84. Walton, S. and J. Huey, *Sam Walton, made in America : my story*. 1st ed. 1992, New York: Doubleday. xiii, 269 p.

85. Kroc, R. and R. Anderson, *Grinding it out : the making of McDonald's*. 1977, Chicago: H. Regnery. 201 p., [8] leaves of plates.

86. Hamel, G. and C.K. Prahalad, *Strategic Intent*. Harvard Business Review, 1989 (May-June): p. 63–76.

87. Bennis, W.G. and B. Nanus, *Leaders : strategies for taking charge*. 2nd ed. 1997, New York: HarperBusiness. xvii, 235 p.

88. Hill, N., *Think and grow rich*. 2007, Mineola, NY: Dover Publications.

89. Beckhard, R. and W. Pritchard, *Changing the essence : the art of creating and leading fundamental change in organizations*. 1st ed. The Jossey-Bass management series. 1992, San Francisco: Jossey-Bass Publishers. xviii, 105 p.

90. Kanter, R.M., *When giants learn to dance*. 1989, New York: Simon and Schuster. 415 p.

91. Drucker, P.F., *The practice of management*. 1st Perennial Library ed. 1986, New York: Perennial Library. xii, 404 p.

92. Porter, M.E., *Competitive advantage : creating and sustaining superior performance : with a new introduction*. 1st Free Press ed. 1998, New York: Free Press. xxiv, 557 p.

93. Davenport, T.H., *Process innovation: reengineering work through information technology*. 1993, Boston, Mass.: Harvard Business School Press. x, 337 p.

94. Thurow, L.C., *Building wealth : the new rules for individuals, companies, and nations in a knowledge-based economy.* 1st ed. 1999, New York: HarperCollins. xvi, 301 p.

95. Drucker, P.F., *Management challenges for the 21st century.* 1st ed. 1999, New York: HarperBusiness. xi, 207 p.

96. Baghai, M., S. Coley, and D. White, *The alchemy of growth : practical insights for building the enduring enterprise.* 1999, Reading, Mass.: Perseus Books. xv, 250 p.

97. Schuller, R.H., *Your church has a fantastic future! : a possibility thinker's guide to a successful church.* 1986, Ventura, Calif.: Regal Books. 359 p.

98. Porter, M.E., *Competitive strategy : techniques for analyzing industries and competitors : with a new introduction.* 1st Free Press ed. 1998, New York: Free Press. xxviii, 396 p.

99. Harvard Business School., *Harvard business essentials : strategy : create and implement the best strategy for your business.* 2005, Boston, Mass.: Harvard Business School Press. xxi, 162 p.

100. Saloner, G., A. Shepard, and J.M. Podolny, *Strategic management.* 2001, New York: John Wiley. xvii, 442 p.

101. Review, H.B., *Michael E. Porter on Competition and Strategy.* 1991, Cambridge, Massachussetts: Harvard Business School. 80 p.

102. Murphy, E.C. and M. Snell, *The genius of Sitting Bull.* 1993, Englewood Cliffs, N.J.: Prentice Hall. xliii, 340 p.

103. Perry, L.T., R.G. Stott, and W.N. Smallwood, *Real-time strategy : improvising team-based planning for a fast-changing world.* The Portable MBA series. 1993, New York: Wiley. xv, 250 p.

104. Davenport, T.H. and L. Prusak, *Information ecology: mastering the information and knowledge environment.* 1997, New York: Oxford University Press. x, 255 p.

105. Ohmae, K.I., *The mind of the strategist.* 1983, New York, NY: Penguin Books. xiii, 283 p.

106. Pfeffer, J., *Competitive advantage through people : unleashing the power of the work force.* 1994, Boston, Mass.: Harvard Business School Press. ix, 281 p.

107. Treacy, M. and F.D. Wiersema, *The discipline of market leaders : choose your customers, narrow your focus, dominate your market.* Expanded ed. 1997, Reading, Mass.: Addison-Wesley Pub. Co. xiv, 210 p.

108. Christensen, C.M. and M.E. Raynor, *The innovator's solution : creating and sustaining successful growth.* 2003, Boston, Mass.: Harvard Business School Press. x, 304 p.

109. Haller, T., *Secrets of the master business strategists.* 1983, Englewood Cliffs, N.J.: Prentice Hall. xiii, 218 p.

110. Keller, K.L., *Strategic brand management : building, measuring, and managing brand equity.* 3rd ed. 2008, Upper Saddle River, N.J.: Pearson/Prentice Hall.

111. Oster, S.M., *Modern competitive analysis.* 3rd ed. 1999, New York: Oxford University Press. x, 434 p.

112. Kochan, N. and Interbrand (Firm), *The world's greatest brands.* 1997, Washington, N.Y.: New York University Press. xxviii, 188 p.

113. McNally, D. and K.D. Speak, *Be your own brand : a breakthrough formula for standing out from the crowd.* 1st ed. 2002, San Francisco, CA: Berrett-Koehler. x, 148 p.

114. Mezirow, J., *Understanding transformation theory.* Adult Education Quarterly, 1994. 44: p. 222–232.

115. Dutton, J.E. and J.M. Dukerich, *Keeping an eye on the mirror : image and identity in organizational adaptation.* The Academy of Management Journal, 1991. 34(3): p. 517–554.

116. Piderit, S.K., *Rethinking resistance and recognizing ambivalence : a multidimensional view of attitudes toward an organizational change.* Academy of Management Review, 2000. 25(4): p. 783–794.

117. Kelly, K., *Out of control : the rise of neo-biological civilization.* 1994, Reading, Mass.: Addison-Wesley. 521 p.

118. Pfeffer, J. and R.I. Sutton, *The knowing-doing gap : how smart companies turn knowledge into action.* 2000, Boston, Mass.: Harvard Business School Press. xv, 314 p.

119. Ackermann, F., C. Eden, and S. Cropper, *Getting started with cognitive mapping,* in *7th Young OR Conference.* 1992: University of Warwick. p. 65–82.

120. Williamson, O.E., S.G. Winter, and R.H. Coase, *The Nature of the firm : origins, evolution, and development.* 1991, New York: Oxford University Press. viii, 235 p.

121. Bennis, W.G., G.M. Spreitzer, and T.G. Cummings, *The future of leadership : today's top leadership thinkers speak to tomorrow's leaders.* The Jossey-Bass business & management series. 2001, San Francisco: Jossey-Bass. xvi, 316 p.

122. Ries, A. and J. Trout, *Positioning : the battle for your mind.* 2001, New York ; London: McGraw-Hill. viii, 213 p.

123. Bonoma, T.V., *The marketing edge : making strategies work*. 1985, New York: Free Press. xiii, 241 p.

124. Goldston, M.R., *The turnaround prescription : repositioning troubled companies*. 1992, New York Toronto: Free Press; Maxwell Macmillan Canada; Maxwell Macmillan International. xix, 198 p.

125. Ries, A. and L. Ries, *The 22 immutable laws of branding : how to build a product or service into a world-class brand*. 1st ed. 2002, New York: HarperBusiness. xvi, 255 p.

126. Aaker, D.A., *Building strong brands*. 1996, New York: Free Press. ix, 380 p.

127. Aaker, D.A. and D. McLoughlin, *Strategic market management*. European ed. 2007, Hoboken, NJ: Wiley.

128. Kotler, P. and K.L. Keller, *Marketing management*. Twelfth ed. 2006, Upper Saddle River, NJ: Pearson Prentice Hall. xxxix, 733 [45] p.

129. Puri, S., *Iso 9000 Certification: Total Quality Management* 1992, Ottawa: Standards Quality Management Group.

130. Peters, T.J. and R.H. Waterman, *In search of excellence : lessons from America's best-run companies*. 2004, New York: HarperBusiness Essentials.

131. Watson, S.R. and D.M. Buede, *Decision synthesis : the principles and practice of decision analysis*. 1987, Cambridge [Cambridgeshire]; New York: Cambridge University Press. xvi, 299 p.

132. Allison, G.T. and P. Zelikow, *Essence of decision : explaining the Cuban Missile Crisis*. 2nd ed. 1999, New York: Longman. xv, 416 p.

133. Ash, M.K., *Miracles happen : the life and timeless principles of the founder of Mary Kay, Inc.* 1st Quill ed. 2003, New York: Quill. xiv, 193 p.

134. Ash, M.K., *Mary Kay on people management.* 1984, New York, N.Y.: Warner Books. xix, 184 p.

135. Keup, E.J., *Franchise bible : how to buy a franchise or franchise your own business.* 6th ed. 2007, [Irvine, CA]: Entrepreneur Press. xvii, 331 p.

136. Sherman, A.J., *Franchising & licensing : two powerful ways to grow your business in any economy.* 3rd ed. 2004, New York: AMACOM. xi, 436 p.

137. Geneen, H. and A. Moscow, *Managing.* 1st ed. 1984, Garden City, N.Y.: Doubleday. x, 297 p.

138. Chopra, D., *The seven spiritual laws of success : a pocketbook guide to fulfilling your dreams.* Abridged ed. 2007, San Rafael, Calif. [S.l.]: Amber-Allen Pub.; Distributed by Hay House, Inc. 96 p.

139. Chopra, D., *The way of the wizard : twenty spiritual lessons in creating the life you want.* 1st ed. 1995, New York: Harmony Books. 169 p.

140. Crum, T.F., *Journey to center : lessons in unifying body, mind, and spirit.* 1997, New York: Simon & Schuster. 222 p.

141. Laozi and S. Mitchell, *Tao te ching : a new English version.* 1st ed. 1988, New York: HarperCollins. xi, 121 p.

142. Castaneda, C., *A separate reality; further conversations with Don Juan.* 1971, New York,: Simon and Schuster. 317 p.

143. Hill, N., *The law of success in sixteen lessons : teaching, for the first time in the history of the world, the true philosophy upon which all personal*

success is built. Facsimile ed. 2000, Chatsworth, Calf.: Wilshire Book Co.

144. Fiol, C.M. and M.A. Lyles, *Organizational learning*. Academy of Management Review, 1985. 10(4): p. 803–813.

145. Levinthal, D.A. and J.G. March, *The myopia of learning*. Strategic Management Journal, 1993. 14: p. 95–112.

146. Levitt, B. and J.G. March, *Organizational learning*. Annual Review of Sociology, 1988. 14: p. 319–340.

147. Porras, J.I., *Stream analysis : a powerful way to diagnose and manage organizational change*. The Addison-Wesley series on organization development. 1987, Reading, Mass.: Addison-Wesley. xvi, 163 p.

148. Nadler, D., M.S. Gerstein, and R.B. Shaw, *Organizational architecture : designs for changing organizations*. 1st ed. The Jossey-Bass management series. 1992, San Francisco: Jossey-Bass. xix, 284 p.

149. Krajewski, L.J. and L.P. Ritzman, *Operations management : strategy and analysis*. 6th ed. 2002, Upper Saddle River, NJ: Prentice Hall. xxv, 883 p.

150. Ballou, R.H., *Business logistics management : planning, organizing, and controlling the supply chain*. 4th ed. 1999, Upper Saddle River, NJ: Prentice Hall. xiv, 681 p.

151. Hayes, R.H., S.C. Wheelwright, and K.B. Clark, *Dynamic manufacturing : creating the learning organization*. 1988, New York, NY: Free Press.

152. Magee, J.F., W.C. Copacino, and D.B. Rosenfield, *Modern logistics management : integrating marketing, manufacturing, and physical*

distribution. Wiley series on marketing management. 1985, New York: Wiley. xi, 430 p.

153. Review, H.B., *The New Manufacturing*. 1991, Cambridge, Massachussetts: Harvard Business School Press.

154. Schonberger, R., *World class manufacturing : the lessons of simplicity applied*. 1986, New York London: Free Press; Collier Macmillan. xi, 252 p.

155. Stock, J.R. and D.M. Lambert, *Strategic logistics management*. 4th ed. The McGraw-Hill/Irwin series in marketing. 2001, Boston: McGraw-Hill/Irwin. xxix, 872 p.

156. Blanchard, B.S., *Logistics engineering and management*. 6th ed. 2004, Upper Saddle River, N.J.: Pearson Prentice Hall. xiii, 564 p.

157. Bowersox, D.J., *Leading edge logistics : competitive positioning for the 1990's : comprehensive research on logistics organization, strategy and behavior in North America*. 1989, Oak Brook, Ill.: Council of Logistics Management. 1 v. (various pagings).

158. Coyle, J.J., E.J. Bardi, and C.J. Langley, *The management of business logistics*. 6th ed. 1996, Minneapolis/St. Paul: West Pub. Co. xix, 631 p.

159. Duncan, T. and S.E. Moriarty, *Driving brand value : using integrated marketing to manage profitable stakeholder relationships*. 1997, New York: McGraw-Hill. xix, 284 p.

160. James, B.G., *Business wargames*. 1st US ed. 1985, Cambridge, Mass.: Abacus Press. ix, 233 p.

161. Hammer, M. and J. Champy, *Reengineering the corporation : a manifesto for business revolution*. 1st HarperBusiness Essentials pbk. ed. 2003, New York: HarperBusiness Essentials. xii, 257 p.

162. Davis, S.M. and W.H. Davidson, *2020 vision*. 1991, New York: Simon & Schuster. 223 p.

163. Stasey, R. and C.J. McNair, *Crossroads : a JIT success story*. The Coopers & Lybrand performance solutions series. 1990, Homewood, Ill.: Dow Jones-Irwin. xii, 290 p.

164. Adair-Heeley, C.B., *The human side of just-in-time : how to make the techniques really work*. 1991, New York, NY: AMACOM. xiii, 319 p.

165. Covey, S.R., *The 7 habits of highly effective people : powerful lessons in personal change*. Rev. ed. 2004, New York: Free Press.

166. Goldratt, E.M., *The goal : a process of ongoing improvement*. 3rd ed. 2004, Burlington, VT: Gower.

167. Getty, J.P., *How to be rich*. 1983, New York: Jove Books. ix, 214 p.

168. Project Management Institute., *A guide to the project management body of knowledge (PMBOK guide)*. 3rd ed. 2004, Newtown Square, Pa.: Project Management Institute, Inc. viii, 388 p.

169. *The Standish Group Report - CHAOS*. 1994, The Standish Group: Boston, MA.

170. Sashkin, M. and M.G. Sashkin, *Leadership that matters : the critical factors for making a difference in people's lives and organizations' success*. 1st ed. 2003, San Francisco: Berrett-Koehler. xi, 241 p.

171. De Pree, M., *Leadership jazz*. 1st ed. 1992, New York: Currency Doubleday. 228 p.

172. Blanchard, K.H., *The heart of a leader*. 1999, Tulsa, Okla: Honor Books. 157 p.

173. Kotter, J.P., *Leading change.* 1996, Boston, Mass.: Harvard Business School Press. x, 187 p.

174. Yukl, G.A., *Leadership in organizations.* 6th ed. 2006, Upper Saddle River, NJ: Pearson/Prentice Hall. xvi, 542 p.

175. Stahl, J., *Lessons on leadership : the 7 fundamental management skills for leaders at all levels.* 2007, New York: Kaplan Pub. xix, 218 p.

176. Patterson, M.L. and S. Lightman, *Accelerating innovation : improving the process of product development.* 1993, New York: Van Nostrand Reinhold. xv, 159 p.

177. Gates, B. and J. Lowe, *Bill Gates speaks : insight from the world's greatest entrepreneur.* 1998, New York: John Wiley. xviii, 253 p.

178. Cusumano, M.A. and R.W. Selby, *Microsoft secrets : how the world's most powerful software company creates technology, shapes markets, and manages people.* 1995, New York: Free Press. xii, 512 p.

179. Gates, B., N. Myhrvold, and P. Rinearson, *The road ahead.* Completely rev. and up-to-date. ed. 1996, New York: Penguin Books. xviii, 332 p.

180. Holmes, O.W., *The one-hoss shay, The chambered nautilus, and other poems, gay and grave.* 1900, Boston and New York,: Houghton, Mifflin and company. viii, 154 p., 1 l.

181. Coase, R.H., *Essays on economics and economists.* 1994, Chicago: University of Chicago Press. viii, 222 p.

182. Drucker, P.F., *Management : tasks, responsibilities, practices.* 2007, New Brunswick, NJ: Transaction Publishers. xvi, 839 p.

183. Smith, D.K. and R.C. Alexander, *Fumbling the future : how Xerox invented, then ignored, the first personal computer.* 1st ed. 1988, New York: W. Morrow. 274 p.

184. Gordon, I., *Relationship marketing : new strategies, techniques, and technologies to win the customers you want and keep them forever.* 1998, Toronto; New York: John Wiley & Sons Canada. xx, 314 p.

185. Segil, L., *Intelligent business alliances : how to profit using today's most important strategic tool.* 1st ed. 1996, New York: Times Business. xx, 251 p.

186. Segil, L., *Fastalliances : power your E-business.* 2001, New York: John Wiley. x, 310 p.

187. Seybold, P.B. and R.T. Marshak, *Customers.com : how to create a profitable business strategy for the Internet and beyond.* 1st ed. 1998, New York: Times Business. xx, 360 p.

188. Bly, R.W., *Keeping clients satisfied: make your service business more successful and profitable.* 1993, Englewood Cliffs, N. J.: Prentice Hall. xi, 275 p.

189. Peppers, D. and M. Rogers, *The one to one manager : real-world lessons in customer relationship management.* 1st ed. 1999, New York: Currency/Doubleday. xix, 268 p.

190. Goleman, D.P., M. Maccoby, and T.H. Davenport, *What makes a good leader.* 2001, Boston, MA: Harvard Business Review.

191. Porch, G. and J. Niederer, *Coach anyone about anything : how to help people succeed in business and life.* 1st. ed. 2002, Del Mar, CA: Wharton Publishing, Inc. p.

192. Blanchard, K.H. and S. Johnson, *The one minute manager*. 10th anniversary ed. 1983, New York: Berkley Books. 111 p.

193. Martin, D. and R. Martin, *Teamthink : using the sports connection to develop, motivate, and manage a winning business team*. 1994, New York: Plume.

194. Fairley, S.G. and C.E. Stout, *Getting started in personal and executive coaching : how to create a thriving coaching practice*. Getting started in. 2004, Hoboken, N.J.: J. Wiley & Sons. x, 356 p.

195. Marquardt, M.J., *Leading with questions : how leaders find the right solutions by knowing what to ask*. 1st ed. 2005, San Francisco: Jossey-Bass. viii, 216 p.

196. Evans, D., *Emotion : the science of sentiment*. 2001, Oxford; New York: Oxford University Press. xvi, 204 p.

197. Arbinger Institute., *Leadership and self-deception: getting out of the box*. 1st ed. 2000, San Francisco: Berrett-Koehler. x, 181 p.

198. Wiskup, M., *The "it" factor : be the one people like, listen to, and remember*. 2007, New York: AMACOM, American Management Association. ix, 179 p.

199. Goleman, D., *Emotional intelligence*. Bantam 10th anniversary hardcover ed. 2006, New York: Bantam Books. xxiv, 358 p.

200. Van Fleet, J.K., *Lifetime conversation guide*. 1984, Englewood Cliffs, N.J.: Prentice-Hall. xxiv, 297 p.

201. Andreas, S., C. Faulkner, and NLP Comprehensive (Organization), *NLP : the new technology of achievement*. 1st ed. 1994, New York: Morrow. 354 p.

202. Schuller, R.H., *Discover Your Possibilities*. 1986, New York, New York: Ballantine Books.

203. Carnegie, D., *How to win friends and influence people*. Rev. ed. 1982, New York: Pocket Books. xxv, 276 p.

204. Gobet, F., et al., *Chunking mechanisms in human learning*. Trends in Cognitive Science, 2001. 5: p. 236–243.

205. Singer, M.T., *Cults in our midst*. Rev. ed. 2003, San Francisco, CA: Jossey-Bass. xxviii, 397 p.

206. Janssen, J., *Championship team building : what every coach needs to know to build a motivated, committed & cohesive team*. 2002, Cary, N.C.: Winning The Mental Game. xvii, 188 p.

207. Miller, J.B. and P.B. Brown, *The corporate coach*. 1st HarperBusiness ed. 1994, New York, NY: HarperBusiness. xv, 235 p.

208. Jones, L.B., *Jesus, CEO : using ancient wisdom for visionary leadership*. 1st ed. 1995, New York: Hyperion. xviii, 318 p.

209. Fiske, S.T. and S.E. Taylor, *Social cognition : from brains to culture*. 1st ed. 2008, Boston: McGraw-Hill Higher Education. xii, 540 p.

210. Wilson, R.A., *Prometheus rising*. 1st ed. 1983, Phoenix, Ariz., U.S.A.: Falcon Press. v, 262 p.

211. Bach, G.L. and R.J. Flanagan, *Macroeconomics : analysis, decision making, and policy*. 11th ed. 1987, Englewood Cliffs, N.J.: Prentice-Hall. xiii, 458 p.

212. Hall, R.E. and J.B. Taylor, *Macroeconomics*. 5th ed. 1997, New York: W.W. Norton & Co. xxiv, 528, 36 p.

213. Eisenhardt, K.M., *Agency theory : an assessment and review.* Academy of Management Review, 1989. 14(1): p. 57–74.

214. Porter, M.E., *The competitive advantage of nations : with a new introduction.* 1998, New York: Free Press. xxxii, 855 p.

215. North, D.C., *Structure and change in economic history.* 1st ed. 1981, New York: Norton. xi, 228 p.

216. Stewart, G.B., *The quest for value : a guide for senior managers.* 1991, [New York, N.Y.]: HarperBusiness. xxvii, 781 p.

217. Marren, J.H., *Mergers & acquisitions : a valuation handbook.* 1993, Homewood, Ill.: Business One Irwin. xxiii, 548 p.

218. Damodaran, A., *Damodaran on valuation : security analysis for investment and corporate finance.* 2nd ed. Wiley finance series. 2006, Hoboken, N.J.: John Wiley & Sons. x, 685 p.

219. Van Horne, J.C. and J.M. Wachowicz, *Fundamentals of financial management.* 11th ed. 2001, Upper Saddle River, N.J.: Prentice Hall. xxi, 743 p.

220. Van Horne, J.C., *Financial management and policy.* 12th ed. Prentice Hall finance series. 2002, Upper Saddle River, N.J.: Prentice Hall. xviii, 814 p.

221. Stewart, T.A., *Intellectual capital : the new wealth of organizations.* 1st ed. 1997, New York: Doubleday/Currency. xxi, 278 p.

222. Gerber, M.E. and P. O'Heffernan, *The E-myth, why most businesses don't work and what to do about it.* 1986, Cambridge, Ma.: Ballinger Pub. xiv, 162 p.

223. Gerber, M.E., *The E-myth revisited : why most small businesses don't work and what to do about it.* 1st ed. 1995, New York, N.Y.: Harper-Business. xvi, 268 p.

224. Swanson, J.A. and M.L. Baird, *Engineering your start-up : a guide for the high-tech entrepreneur.* 2nd ed. 2003, Belmont, CA: Professional Publications. xxx, 447 p.

225. Pollan, S.M. and M. Levine, *The field guide to starting a business.* 1990, New York: Simon & Schuster. 255 p.

226. Harrell, W., *For entrepreneurs only.* 1995, Franklin Lakes, NJ: Career Press. 223 p.

227. Nelson, R.P., *The design of advertising.* 7th ed. 1994, Madison, Wis.: Brown & Benchmark. ix, 413 p.

228. Collins, J.C. and J.I. Porras, *Built to last : successful habits of visionary companies.* 1st ed. 1994, New York: HarperBusiness. xiv, 322 p.

229. Lipnack, J. and J. Stamps, *The age of the network : organizing principles for the 21st century.* 1994, New York: Wiley. xx, 264 p.

230. Slywotzky, A.J., D. Morrison, and K. Weber, *How digital is your business?* 1st ed. 2000, New York: Crown Business. viii, 327 p.

231. Davis, S.M. and C. Meyer, *Blur : the speed of change in the connected economy.* 1998, Reading, Mass.: Addison-Wesley. xiii, 265 p.

232. Levine, R., *The cluetrain manifesto : the end of business as usual.* 2000, Cambridge, Mass.: Perseus Books. xxii, 190 p.

233. Hutchinson, S.E. and S.C. Sawyer, *Computers and information systems*, in *Irwin advantage series for computer education.* 1994, Richard D. Irwin, Inc.: Burr Ridge, Ill. p. v.

234. Kalakota, R. and M. Robinson, *E-Business : roadmap for success.* Addison-Wesley information technology series. 1999, Reading, Mass.: Addison-Wesley. xvii, 378 p.

235. Kempis, R.-D., *Do IT smart : seven rules for superior information technology performance.* 1st Free Press ed. 1999, New York: Free Press. xii, 211 p.

236. Madnick, S.E., *The Strategic use of information technology.* The Executive Bookshelf. 1987, New York: Oxford University Press. xiii, 206 p.

237. Tapscott, D., et al., *Blueprint to the digital economy ; creating wealth in the era of e-business.* 1998, New York: McGraw-Hill. xxi, 410 p.

238. Coffield, F., et al., *Learning stlyles and pedagogy in post-16 learning : a systematic and critical review.* 2004, Learning and Skills Research Centre: London.

239. Myers, I.B. and M.H. McCaulley, *A guide to the development and use of the Myers-Briggs type indicator.* 1998, Palo Alto: CA: Consulting Psychologists Press.

240. Keirsey, D., *Please understand me II : temperament, character, intelligence.* 1st ed. 1998, Del Mar, CA: Prometheus Nemesis. 350 p.

241. Lopker, J., *Pictures of personality : guide to the four human natures.* 1st ed. 2000, Los Angeles, CA: Typology. 200 p.

242. Ford, N. and S.Y. Chen, *Matching/mismatching revisited : an empirical study of learning and teaching styles.* British Journal of Educational Technology, 2001. 32(1): p. 5–22.

243. Garland, D. and B. Martin, *Do gender and learning style play a role in how online courses should be designed?* Journal of Interactive Online Learning 2005. 4(2): p. 4–9.

244. Zhenhui, R., *Matching teaching styles with learning styles in east asian contexts.* The Internet TESL Journal, 2001. 11(7).

245. Spender, J.C., *Making knowledge the basis of a dynamic theory of the firm.* Strategic Management Journal, 1996. 17(Special Issue: Knowledge amd the Firm): p. 46–62.

246. Weiner, R., *Professional's guide to publicity.* 1975, New York: Weiner. 133 p.

247. Buford, B., *Halftime : changing your game plan from success to significance.* 1994, Grand Rapids, Mich.: Zondervan. 175 p.

248. Buford, B., *Game plan : winning strategies for the second half of your life.* 1997, Grand Rapids, Mich.: Zondervan. 170 p.

ABOUT THE AUTHOR

Jack Bergstrand is a leading expert on Enterprise reinvention and knowledge work productivity, specializing in business change efforts that have significant information technology components. After a two-decade career in the Coca-Cola system, including leading and restructuring The Coca-Cola Company's global information technology function, he founded Brand Velocity, Inc., a company that uses knowledge work productivity principles to accelerate large Enterprise projects. Jack has a master's degree in management from the Stanford Graduate School of Business, a master's in advertising from Michigan State University, and is a doctoral candidate at The George Washington University in Executive Leadership.

GLOSSARY

Balance Sheet: A financial report that tracks an Enterprise's assets and liabilities. Similar to owning a house, the difference between the value of the assets and the liabilities is equity.

Beyond their knitting: An expression for when someone moves beyond his or her area of expertise.

Board of Directors: Governs Enterprises for owners and other stakeholders, including choosing the CEO, approving strategic plans and budgets, and overseeing audits and compensation.

Brand Velocity, Inc.: A company prototyped using knowledge work productivity principles and the knowledge work productivity system. The company specializes in accelerated Enterprise projects.

BUILD: The third step of the knowledge work productivity system. It has an "objective work" orientation and is focused on *How* work can best be done.

Capital Investments: Money that companies spend on purchasing or creating assets that have long lives, including buildings, trucks, and large information systems.

CEO: Chief executive officer. The top job in a company. The CEO has responsibility for the firm's strategy, performance, shareholders, employees, and other key stakeholders.

CFO: Chief financial officer. Oversees the financial affairs of a company. The CFO has responsibility for the company's accounting, tax, treasury, and investor relations.

CIO: Chief information officer. Responsible for overseeing computer related operations in companies—including software, hardware, networks, and data security. In some cases CIO also refers to a chief investment officer.

Cognitive Mapping: A modeling technique for drawing diagrams of, and making connections between, the mental models that individuals and groups possess on specific topics.

Contingency Process: A holistic Enterprise technology project management method for the board, executive management, project team, consulting systems integrator, and software owner to manage accelerated projects.

COO: Chief operating officer. The top operating job of a company. The COO has responsibility for the day to day performance of the company's business units.

Cybernetic Hierarchy: Sociologist Talcott Parsons' application of cybernetics to social systems through his General Theory of Action—tied to adaptation, goals, integration, and motivation.

Cybernetic Management: A subjective and objective process to manage knowledge work productivity using the Envision-Design-Build-Operate knowledge work productivity system.

Cybernetics: The science of relationships, control, and organization. It was developed by mathematician Norbert Wiener in 1948 to facilitate self-steering.

DESIGN: The second step of the knowledge work productivity system. It has an "objective knowledge" orientation and is focused on *What* needs to be done *When*.

Detached Engagement: A leadership approach that combines a consistent and unemotional focus on the overall vision and problem solving, with a sense of urgency on day-to-day goals.

Economic Profit: The profit that a company generates less a charge for the assets that it takes to generate the profit, since the firm's asset investment is an opportunity cost.

Economic Value Added: The change in economic profit from year to year.

Enterprise Projects: Large initiatives that benefit from the knowledge work productivity system and independent facilitation—to manage constraints and improve speed and quality.

Entrepreneur: An opportunistic leader who manages the risks and rewards associated with being commercially successful on one hand and going out of business on the other.

ENVISION: The first step of the knowledge work productivity system. It has a "subjective knowledge" orientation and is focused on *Where* the Enterprise intends to go and *Why*.

Face Validity: An expression for when an idea or concept has validity on the surface, based on common sense or previous experience.

Financial Assets: Companies have liquid assets such as cash and fixed assets such as buildings. Intangible assets such as intellectual property are tracked on the balance sheet if money has been paid for them.

Free Cash Flow: This is the money that a company ultimately generates after all of its cash expenses. It's similar to having money left over from your paycheck after all bills are paid.

Functionitis: A condition where the interests of an Enterprise's function—such as marketing, finance, etc.—takes priority over the Enterprise as a whole.

Grandmaster: The highest title that a chess player can receive from the world chess organization.

Herrmann Brain Dominance Instrument®: A survey-based assessment for thinking preferences, based on a metaphoric model of the human brain developed by Ned Herrmann.

Income Statement: A financial report that tracks the revenue, expenses, and profit of an Enterprise. It is also referred to as a P&L (profit and loss) statement.

Information Age: The age of the computer—where people and organizations use machines to store, manipulate, and transmit data and information.

JIT: Just In Time. A management approach used to first reduce inventory to help optimize a manufacturing system, and then use the optimized system to permanently reduce inventory levels.

Keystone Cops: A series of silent movie comedies in the early 1900s featuring an incompetent group of policemen.

Knowledge Age: The era where knowledge is the most important factor of production and where knowledge work productivity improvement is the most important focus of management.

Knowledge Technologist: Person who earns a living through combining manual work and knowledge work to achieve tasks, including a skilled tradesperson and a medical technician.

Knowledge Work: Work that uses ideas, expertise, information, and relationships to achieve tasks. It includes brainstorming, analysis, project management, and personal coaching.

Knowledge Workers: Those who earn a living through knowledge work, including researchers, analysts, managers, consultants, and others who use knowledge to achieve tasks.

Knowledge Work Productivity: The effectiveness and efficiency of knowledge workers to create, improve, and discontinue products, services, activities, and processes.

Knowledge Work Productivity System: The framework and process to manage knowledge work productivity based on the work of Drucker, Burrell, Morgan, Wiener, and Parsons.

Leadership: The ability to successfully move people to a higher vision and a higher level of performance—grounded in strong management practices and high integrity.

Management: The practice of organizing people to achieve better results as a group than they can attain as individuals to help customers lower their costs and be more successful.

Management By Objectives: A management approach originated by Peter F. Drucker, where specific objectives are used to focus the efforts and measures of individuals and the overall Enterprise.

Manual Work: Work that uses the human body and physical tools to achieve tasks. It includes factory work, construction work, and the physical movement of goods.

Manual Workers: Those who earn a living through manual work, including assembly line and warehouse employees, truck drivers, and others who primarily use physical abilities to achieve tasks.

Manual Work Productivity: The effectiveness and efficiency of manual workers to objectively achieve specifically-designed physical tasks.

Market Value: The value of a company's shares—similar to owning $100,000 equity in a $200,000 house. The equity *and* debt of a company, or house, is its total (Enterprise) value.

Mental Model: Frameworks that people have in their minds to interpret the world. Such as, don't touch fire because it hurts. They are invisible by nature but determine many behaviors.

Myers-Briggs Type Indicator®: A psychometric survey to assess how people perceive the world using psychological types developed by Swiss psychiatrist Carl Jung.

9-to-5: A description for the time between 9 am and 5 pm, or 09:00 and 17:00.

OPERATE: The fourth step of the knowledge work productivity system. It has a "subjective work" orientation and focuses on *Who* should be responsible for which tasks.

Operating Profit: The money that a company earns after all of its day-to-day expenses, before paying its taxes and interest payments on loans.

Paradigm: A school of thought that uses a single lens to view a collection of theories (e.g. the sociological Functionalist Paradigm or the Design work-behavior area).

Parkinson's Law: Cyril Northcote Parkinson's notion that work expands to fill the available time and that there is a natural tendency for staff to accumulate.

Peter Principle: Laurence J. Peter's and Raymond Hull's principle that people rise to their level of incompetence in organizational hierarchies.

Productivity: The combination of effectiveness and efficiency. It is measured as output divided by input in the short term and prosperity over the long run.

Productivity Paradox: The observation, with some even considering it a theory, that massive investments in information technology have not resulted in productivity increases.

Property Rights: The right of an individual or group to legally own something and to do with it whatever they choose—while also excluding others from owning it.

Return on Assets: The size of your profits relative to the assets that it takes to generate them. A $1,000 profit on a $10,000 piece of equipment generates a 10% return on assets.

Scientific Management: Objective management techniques developed by Frederick Taylor, and a book by the same title, to improve manual work productivity in the 20th century.

SG&A%: Selling, General & Administrative expense percentage. This measures the percent of day-to-day operating expenses required to generate the company's revenue.

Shareholders: Individuals and firms owning an Enterprise. Their shares make up the company's market value, which is influenced by the profitability and growth of the Enterprise.

Skin in the Game: An expression for when someone is committed to something to the degree that they have something to lose if it's not successful.

Social Sciences: The study of people, as individuals and groups, including academic branches of study including economics, sociology, psychology, and political science.

Strategic Profiling®: Knowledge work productivity instrument for managing accelerated Enterprise projects. It was developed using this book's knowledge work productivity system.

Supply Chain: The movement of goods from suppliers to customers. It includes procurement, manufacturing, warehousing, and distribution functions.

System: A whole—whether mechanical, natural, or social—structure with interdependent parts. As such, the improvement of a single part will not improve the whole if it is not a constraint.

System Dynamics: An important modeling technique created by Jay Forrester and popularized by Peter Senge. It emphasizes the important effect of time delays and feedback loops on systems.

The Complete Process®: Trademark for the knowledge work productivity system described in this book, owned by Brand Velocity, Inc.

The Earning Organization®: Trademark for the knowledge work productivity book series—of which *Reinvent Your Enterprise* is the first book—as well as associated research and consulting.

24/7: A description for twenty-four hours a day and seven days a week.

Virtuous Cycle: Describes when one good activity or event encourages a series of other positive outcomes. This is sometimes also referred to as a "virtuous circle."

Work-behavior Areas: The four steps—Envision-Design-Build-Operate—in the knowledge work productivity system.

INDEX

Brand Velocity, Inc.

3455 Peachtree Road NE, Suite 500

Atlanta, Georgia 30326

www.brandvelocity.com

reinvent@brandvelocity.com

2597448

Made in the USA